Door in the Mountain

WESLEYAN POETRY

DOOR in the MOUNTAIN

New and Collected Poems, 1965–2003

JEAN VALENTINE

WESLEYAN UNIVERSITY PRESS • MIDDLETOWN, CONNECTICUT

for Pesha & Rebecca

with love

Published by Wesleyan University Press, Middletown, CT 06459
This collection © 2004 by Jean Valentine
Printed in the United States of America

5   4   3   2

Library of Congress Cataloging-in-Publication Data

Valentine, Jean.
Door in the mountain : new and collected poems, *1965–2003* / Jean Valentine.
    p.   cm.—(Wesleyan poetry)
Includes indexes.
ISBN 0–8195–6712–4 (cloth : alk. paper)
I. Title. II. Series.
PS3572.A39D66 2004
811'.54—dc22   2004016019

Contents

DREAM BARKER (1965)   39

THE CRADLE OF THE REAL LIFE (2000)   245

Acknowledgments

The following sections of this volume were previously published as books.

Dream Barker. Copyright © 1965 by Yale University Press. Reprinted with the permission of Yale University Press.

Pilgrims. Copyright © 1965, 1966, 1967, 1968, 1969 by Jean Valentine. First published by Farrar, Straus & Giroux in 1969.

Ordinary Things. Copyright © 1972, 1973, 1974 by Jean Valentine. First published by Farrar, Straus & Giroux in 1974.

The Messenger. Copyright © 1974, 1975, 1976, 1977, 1978, 1979 by Jean Valentine. First published by Farrar, Straus & Giroux in 1979.

Home.Deep.Blue. Copyright © 1980, 1981, 1982, 1983, 1984, 1985, 1986, 1987, 1988, 1989 by Jean Valentine. Reprinted with the permission of Alice James Books.

The River at Wolf. Copyright © 1992 by Jean Valentine. Reprinted with the permission of Alice James Books.

Growing Darkness, Growing Light. Copyright © 1997 by Jean Valentine. First published by Carnegie Mellon University Press in 1997.

The Cradle of the Real Life. Copyright © 2000 by Jean Valentine.

Grateful acknowledgment is made to the following periodicals in which the poems in *Door in the Mountain* first appeared: *American Poetry Review, Arts & Letters, Barrow Street, Boston Book Review, <canwehaveourballback .com>, Hayden's Ferry, Heliotrope, Kestrel, Luna, Massachusetts Review, The New Yorker* ("Sheep," "My old body," "One Foot in the Dark"); *Ohio Review, Persephone, Poetry Ireland, Two Rivers, U.S. 1 Worksheets, van Gogh's Ear, Virginia Quarterly Review,* and *Washington Square Review.*

Also to the following anthologies: *Best American Poems 2002, Blood and Tears: Poems for Matthew Shepard, The Book of Irish American Poetry, Hammer and Blaze,* and *Poetry After 9/11.*

To the editors, and to Dorland Mountain, The MacDowell Colony, and Yaddo, my deep thanks.

New Poems

Annunciation

I saw my soul become flesh   breaking open
the linseed oil breaking over the paper
running down   pouring
no one to catch it   my life breaking open
no one to contain it   my
pelvis thinning out into God

*

In our child house

In our child house
our mother read to us:
England:
            there the little
English boy would love us under
neath a tree:
            not kill us:
that was white space only
like her childhood   like her
father   her sorrow

Nine

Your hand on my knee
I couldn't move

The heat felt good
I couldn't move

The shutmouth mother goes down the stairs
and drinks warm whiskey

she always goes
and drinks warm whiskey

down in the corner: Hand-
me-down:

And everything on the hair
of starting again.

The girl

spills the half-gallon of milk on the floor.
The milk is all over the floor, the table,
the chairs, the books, the dinner, the windows

—Mother and son are gone happy.
The father to work.
The sister to marriage.

The girl is still spilling
the milk-house
white negative shining
out of one life into another life.

Mother

in your white dress
your smoke
your opaque eye

you whose name
my foot
wrote

I had to die
break the rope
push through the stone fence

of you, of myself, and fly

Eighteen

Green bookbag full of poems
I leaned with my bicycle
at the black brick edge of the world

What was I, to be lost
or found?

My soul in the corner
stood
watched

*

Girl and boy
we had given each other
we wanted   breasts
bellies   hair
toenails   fingernails
hair   nipples
foreskin   foreskin
heart

*

I gave up signing in
to the night book
little notes in time

signing our names
on the train's engine car
gray 19th century Irish men
in our gray stiff clothes

"She Sang"

Save the goat of humanity!
She started out
shot through with love books

She chose closed hearts
those she knew
would not kill her

Save her memory   her bones
dig under the house
dig near home

here at the X in the mouth of the house
the shell shocked woman   all her bones
goat bones

A Bone Standing Up

A bone standing up
she worked for words
word by word
up Mt. Fear till
she got to her name: it was
"She Sang."

The Hawthorn Robin Mends with Thorns

Talking with Mary about 1972:
like a needle
through my 25-years-
older breast my years thinner rib: 1972:

a child-life
away from my children:

"but you couldn't have been different
from the way you were"

but I *would* to have been different

Out in a sailboat

Out in a sailboat with the warden
he says so-and-so weighs 95 lbs. now
says she slept with him
because he was kind
when she was in prison

She woke up
hypnotized

A wonderful boat

She woke up
walking with the homeless
on a plank
no red schlock rope

I came to you

I came to you
Lord, because of
the fucking *reticence*
of this world
no, not the *world*, not *reticence*, oh
    Lord Come
    Lord Come
We were sad on the ground
    Lord Come
We were sad on the ground.

*

Cousin

The erotic brown fedora on the desk:
the erotic silver watch from your father's time
balanced on its thin hinged silver lid
on the Teacher's Desk:

Once or twice, someone comes along
and you stand up in the air
and the air rises up out of the air:

One leaf
then branches
stood up in the sun consuming
—Cousin, it was happiness on earth.

The Very Bad Horse

The very bad horse doesn't budge until the pain penetrates to the marrow of its bones.
—The Buddha

My first own home
my big green "bed-sit"
in London, in 1956
double bed   green spread
sixpence coin-fed gas fire
London fog   huge little footsteps
TOK TOK TOK

I knew three people
and three more at work
I knew you

I felt around in the dark for Life
and you   I picked myself up by the hair
four stories up and dropped me

—Still I wouldn't budge.

Once

Once there was a woodcutter,
when he asked me to marry him
the woman in the grocery store said
You look like you lost your last friend.
First love!
When we broke up
it was as if the last egg in the house
got dropped on the broken floor.
     This world is everywhere! the woman said,
     You won't go unsampled!

So many secrets

So many secrets
held you in their glass

Fear
like a green glass
on the shelf

It hurt like glass
It hurt like self

Eleventh Brother

one arm still a swan's wing
The worst had happened before: love—before
I knew it was mine—
turned into a wild
swan   and flew
across the rough water

Outsider   seedword
until I die
I will be open to you as an egg
speechless red

Once in the nights

Once in the nights
I raced through fast
snow to drink life
from a shoe

what I thought
was wrong with me   with you
was not wrong
                    now
gates in the dark at thy name hinge

Under the gold

Under the gold and chalk and brick, beside
the rowers on the river,

the black lines lived around my crayon bones.
One line.   And then my heart shut down,

even so, inside the lines.   I rode
out of the sorrowfence   blue

twine-tied gate
into the river grass . . .

The Windows

Funeral dream
"We'll put them all down in the great book of sleep."

"You may be dead but
Don't stop loving me."

In memory
"Don't hold yourself cheap."

All the windows came to him in tears.

The chestnut tree by the North River. Its tears.

Dream   A bricklayer.   Your father.

Dream   "If you shoot someone
I will walk out on the ocean floor
and throw the gun away."

Dream   "When I am of doubt . . ."
Dream   "Go clear."

Go Clear

Go clear   he said
              his high gray 19th c.
              postmortem jaw
              I loved it   its high grayness

go clear   no touch
              but words   no more
              death fear

I swam   out of the streaming ikon eyes
              who loved me: not-me: no more care
              I left the clothes
              standing there   I swam

into swarming projectless air
redemptionless
from under the earth to over the earth
air   to   not air

The Coin

While you were alive
and thought well of me
there was always a coin in my fish-mouth
off in the night
or the day lake. Now
the little coin doesn't need itself . . .

October morning

October morning—
sea lions barking
on the off-shore rock

Autumn evening—
seals' heads nosing through
the pink Pacific

I gather myself
onto my day raft, your voice
lost under me:
first other tongue

I heard my left hand

I heard my left hand love for my right hand
white through the screen door

just as through the summer elm   you
two years ago   in the bardo

moved into the room *we* once had feeling for.

In the evening

In the evening
I saw them

their little
open boats

carrying us
across the blood water

their invisible company
their invisible company

you beauty   I never
did not know

no time
no place

you beauty
little ferryman

*

We cut the new day

We cut the new day
like a key:
betrayal:

We went ahead anyway
drinking down the will of the event

On the eighth floor
something fell
alive inside the old street wall
next to the bed

I heard it fall
and fall

Occurrence of White

First thriving, then failing to thrive:
no never thriving,
from the beginning,
the ghost freighter out of Fall River,
ghost railroad car out of Chicago,
raked my skin and your skin in white silence.

How have I hurt you?

How have I hurt you?
  You saw me.

I dream I *am* you
full of fear and dread
with me in your arms
:my cloth love
holding your breath

How have I hurt you
  You saw me

I didn't see you

  Do flies remember us

Do flies remember us
We don't them
we say "fly"

say
"woman"
"man"

you   gone
through my hands
me through your hands

our footprints feeling
over us
thirstily

  You drew my head

You drew my head
the back of my head
my neck stem

you made my head a charcoal skull
and even the skull
is turned away

no eyes

The little, faintly blue clay eggs

The little, faintly blue clay eggs
in the real grass nest you made and sent to me
by hand:
          It runs through my thighs, even now,
that you *thought* of it!
for a little while we thought of nothing else.
Frozen little couple in caps,
frozen beaks—

Happiness (3)

The moment you turned to me on W. 4th St.
Your gentleness to me

The hard winter grass here under my shoes
The frost

I knelt in the frost to your parents

                        The warm
light on the right hand side of your face
The light on the Buddha's eyelids

I knelt to my parents
Their suffering   How

much sleep there was in sleep   How no
suffering is lost

Letter

The hornet holds on to the curtain, winter
sleep. Rubs her legs. Climbs the curtain.
Behind her the cedars sleep lightly,

like guests. But I am the guest.
The ghost cars climb the ghost highway. Even my hand
over the page   adds to the 'room tone': the little

constant wind. The effort of becoming. These words
are my life. The effort
of loving the un-become. To make the suffering

visible. The un-become love: What we
lost, a leaf, what we cherish, a leaf.
One leaf of grass. I'm sending you this seed-pod,

this red ribbon, my tongue,
these two red ribbons, my mouth, my other mouth,

—but the other world—blindly I guzzle
the swimming milk of *its* seed field flower—

I could never let go

my husband
my wound
my sleep

but they were surrendered from me

my books   them
pleasing you/
disappointing you

the desire for men
gazing
feeding

the cursive characters
I   *my*
you

in chalk across
the white-lined blackboard

surrendered from me
when I couldn't breathe so.

The Basket House

The basket house:
to shelter me
inside the night cave
the emptiness
where the other one holds me

nurses me
in the emptiness,

holds me the way
paper   made out of a tree
holds a deer.

And he holds me near:
he pulls the cord
out from me, in to him,
length over length.

The House and the World

All this anger
heart beating

unless I'd come inside
your blind window
and stay there like you

But then
the other world
was going to be given:

the cello part
carrying us the whole time

like earth   the scarred hip

tipped groin

the flying whitethorn hedge

the cup

In your eyes

In your eyes
there was a little pupil

a woman
turned to
a holy well

notes and snapshots pinned to her dress
at her feet
crutches   eyeglasses

Woman, Leaving

You waited 4 Ever

    Don't listen for words here
no more than the words the grass speaks or
the mouth of the lake

    Then came
an undone stitch of light
You tore it
open and flew

Trim my hoofs

Trim my hoofs!
I am thirsty for experience.

The glass man
on the glass river says

If only I could get
down it alone   —But
you are getting down it alone . . .

Thirsty! I drink
from my own well
the red and blue fire
around my head
this minute
vanishing   I
befriended with it

Two Poems for Matthew Shepard

But what about the blue dory—the soul

—*Thief the sun*   *Thief the rain*

Into love
the size of a silver dollar
[the soul] disappeared
to a pencil point then
nothing.
        Left
his nails
and his hair.

The Blue Dory, the Soul

—I left the blue dory
there had been so much news

so many flashbulbs   breaking
up the dory

so many people
following their names
eating their third heavy car
their third book

I left the blue dory
on its hip   on the fence
left my soul   not "mine"
"my" clothes   off
I left the edges of "my" face
"my" hands

The Rally

The rally is about a young black man
His tongue has been cut by a razor
the tops of his ears have been cut off

My clothes   my bag
my money   my papers
                              It's
the young man

My palms
my soles
              It's
the young man

    your silent invisible body here at the door
    your glance

The Growing Christ of Tzintzuntzan

Come in
at the narrow door, and then
go back, but
          not yet—

Lie down,

head to my bandaged head, foot
to growing foot,
I am so tired, too,
in my glass box.

Sheep

With the winter and mud and shit roped into your wool,
Your black stick legs, blank eyes—
The farmer stumps home to his supper
And you are beyond your own bells
And my friend is in pain and there's nothing I can do,
Suffering is everywhere intense, and if
We make our own pain ourselves, who can help it? Cold selves,
Cold you, unbearable clamor and rust—

To the Bardo

I dreamed I finally got through to C on the phone
he was whispering
I couldn't make out the words

he had been in the hospital
and then in a home
M was sick too

You know how in dreams you are everyone:
awake too you are everyone:
I am listening   breathing your ashy breath

old Chinese poet:
fire:
to see the way

Rodney Dying (4)

A woman was picking up the plastic
forks and napkins in a plastic box
I was sitting on the grass floor leaning
against your knees: Under the ground
I sat down on the floor and embraced your knees.

*

Door in the Mountain

Never ran this hard through the valley
never ate so many stars

I was carrying a dead deer
tied on to my neck and shoulders

deer legs hanging in front of me
heavy on my chest

People are not wanting
to let me in

Door in the mountain
let me in

Monarch butterfly

Monarch butterfly,
dip your hand
in the wooden box
of papers on my back
and open me   Take
the hand inside the hand
I'm struggling to leave:
Let my hand play!

My old body

My old body:
a ladder of sunlight,
mercury dust floating through—

My forgivenesses,
how you have learned to love me in my sleep.

Inkwell   daybreak

Inkwell   daybreak
stairway
            stairway

Dear girls and boys,
would you go with me and tell me
back to the beginning
—so we can understand!
the journey of our lives
where we met with cruelty
but kindness, too,
and nosed up out
of the cold dark water,
and walked on our fins . . .

The path between

The path between the two twelve-foot hedges
between the fire and the window
hot on the left side   sharp on the right
something wrong   Born wrong
cleaves to itself   deflects you
Still, someone wrote something here in the dirt
and I sip at the word—

The Night Sea

The longing for touch
was what they lived out of
not mainly their bodies

For that friend
we walked   inside of the night sea
shedding our skins—

The Shirt

The shirt was going to be red:
he had to have this shirt—no other—
to stay alive, in prison.
We were setting about to cut, and sew,

but the cotton, they said, was sacred
—we had to fold it and give it back to them.
Then, even though you're so much lighter, and it was white,
you gave him yours . . .

One Foot in the Dark

People forget
Don't forget me
                         You
the only white head
in the crowd of young men
live oaks
waiting to be let out of the Visiting Area.

A weed   green

A weed   green
with a black shadow village under it

and then browngray dirt   then a browngray stick
stuck on a stone
which has its own black shoah moat to the north
how hungrily life   like an *o*
goes after life

Fears: Night Cabin

Snake   tick
black widow
brown recluse

—The truck last night on 79
dragging a chain

—A cloud
rounding slowly
at the window

—The wick   unlit
curled cold in the kerosene lamp.

so wild

        so wild
I didn't notice for a long time
under your ten skins
your skull

—When life
for the fourth time touched my eyes

with mud and spit
and groaned

       —Then
I saw your and my fingerbones
outstretching in the thin blue planet water.

    I have lived in your face

I have lived in your face.
Have I *been* you?
Your mother?   giving you birth

—this pain
whenever I say goodbye to thee

—up to now I always wanted it
but not this

    A goldfinch in the rain

A goldfinch in the rain
a broken bird-feeder on the branch above her
its roof an inverted V   without any floor
uncradle rocking

In the Visiting Area:
rocking:
not touching

The grain of the wood

The grain of the wood
tidemarks on the beach
galaxies
fingerprints

The spark inside my ribcage
leaping at your voice
under my skin   and away in the knuckley powder . . .

The push or fly

The push or fly of the snow
here in the free woods

Your letter last night
—lost eight weeks in the prison anthrax rules—
and who knows what push/fly
at Avenal—

". . . mostly freezing weather
and they don't give you anything warm to wear . . ."
at Avenal,

            if I could,
I would nurse you . . .   as I have,
as you have me, spring weather.

I would be

I would be thick soft fleece
around your shoulders
your ill heart   at Avenal

a circle around your head
quiet against the noise, shade from the lights

Avalon

Avalon,
isle of the dead, in the west, where heroes go
after they die—
               Avenal
where do your young men go?
hot coal in no one's mouth, dying day by day
to Avenal—

Do you remember?

Do you remember? my mouth black and blue
from your starved mouth—
I didn't know anything. I didn't know I was from
the way life was before . . . your fire skin
soft as a horse's black muzzle,
soft, soft black hair
of love, white hair on your head
    —Now they have muzzled you.

That life, we couldn't stop, the sun went down,
spring snow was coming was coming

Advent Calendar

In the tiny window for December 21st,
the shortest day,

a little soldier, puppet on a stick,
or is the stick his sword? He looks quite gay.

Out my window, the woods: terrarium:
I put bread on the snow there yesterday,
but no one has come to eat it. It has frozen.
(Easy for them to follow was the child's way.)

Love they could never put you on a stick.
They could kill you in their prison
but they could never have you.

They can do anything.

We didn't know each other

We didn't know each other,
only what we ourselves hardly knew,
though they hurt us, every breath,
the holes in our sides,
though they were invisible,
underground rivers, caves—

Touch with your finger

Touch with your finger
the left side of my chest I hunch to protect
the side that holds like a womb your walking
your walking over to us
at our plastic table in the Visiting Area
your hair cut, your chest caved in,
your face caved in, your covered-over
silence.

Noon in the Line Outside

The pretty woman with a prisoner number, CDCP *****, written in
ballpoint on the palm of her hand. "You have to give them the
number." "You can't bring anything inside." "I'll hold your
place in the line while you go back to the car." Her clear
plastic pocketbook full of quarters for the vending machines inside.
"It has to be clear plastic." "You're allowed $30. in quarters."
I find his number, with the prison pen I write it on the palm of my hand.

Inside

Your red eye—
soap, you said
—injury?
and the darkness
around your eye
and down your cheek
—birthmark? injury?
Close close you drew me in,
Injury—

Your number is lifting off my hand

Your number is lifting off my hand
you are becoming gone

to me   but
the cut-out hurts

where you were
behind my eye

around your eye
down my cheek,

Ancient Injury—

*

The Needle North

I had a boat
lost the food
and the shoes

Hollow wrist
fill it with food
fill it with shoes

Some say we rise like dots into the sky
Walking through the snow
the world begins to whirl

from this immortal coil
to that immortal coil

We whirl now into deadwood
but fire inside
                dead wood but fire

The Passing

The shimmer
gone
out of what we know

Bells
din dan dawn
but we—down here—you little

Lord
the needle North
and move the boat

In the Burning Air

In the burning air
nothing.

But on the ground, at the edge,
a woman and her spoon,
a wooden spoon,
and her chest, the broken
bowl.

      *

She would long
to dig herself into the ground, her only
daughter's ashes
in her nose   in her mouth   her only daughter's
makeshift ashes
nothing
lying
in the hole in her chest

But her eye would still see
up   into   the ground above her, still see
the upper air

—Let her lie down now, snake in her hole, house
snake in her hold.

Little house

Little house
clay house

thousands of funeral smell
ground swell

we *knew*
the boat of right action

but the road rubbed out
—water gone!

—the dead girl gone!
(*was* she pregnant?)

dishes blew by
I searched my hollows   rubble

Burnt grass   teach me
before I forget you

into a time
when I sit and roar

over the flowers
and don't know them

Notes

NEW POEMS

Page 3, "Annunciation": drawn from Helene Aylon's *Breakings*.

Page 5, "Occurrence of White": the first line echoes Jane Kenyon's poem *Things*.

Page 26, "My old body":

> My old body
>   a drop of dew
>   heavy at the leaf tip.
>   —Kiba

Dream Barker

(1965)

First Love

How deep we met in the sea, my love,
My double, my Siamese heart, my whiskery,
Fish-belly, glue-eyed prince, my dearest black nudge,
How flat and reflective my eye reflecting you
Blue, gorgeous in the weaving grasses
I wound round for your crown, how I loved your touch
On my fair, speckled breast, or was it my own turning;
How nobly you spilled yourself across my trembling
Darlings: or was that the pull of the moon,
It was all so dark, and you were green in my eye,
Green above and green below, all dark,
And not a living soul in the parish
Saw you go, hélas!
Gone your feathery nuzzle, or was it mine,
Gone your serpentine
Smile wherein I saw my maidenhood smile,
Gone, gone all your brackish shine,
Your hidden curl, your abandoned kill,
Aping the man, liebchen! my angel, my own!
How deep we met, how dark,
How wet! before the world began.

For a Woman Dead at Thirty

No one ever talked like that before, like your
Last white rush in the still light of your
Last, bungled fever: no one will any more.

Now we breathe easier: Love,
Released from itself, blows words of love all over,
Now your hands are crossed down there.

We wanted your whole body behind glass,
And you left just half a footprint,
Half-smiling.

All night, driving,
I wanted to know:
At the turn of light that somewhere
Must still be cock's crow

You smiled slantwise in the side mirror,
Six months dead: *here's Romance*:
You wanted to know.

You Never, you blazing
Negative, o you wavering light in water,
Water I stir up with a stick: wavering rot,

O my sister!
    even if I'd known,
All I could have said was that I know.

Miles from Home

Grown, and miles from home, why do I shy
From every anonymous door-slam or dull eye?
The giant-step, the yawn
That streaked my dreams twenty years ago are gone;
The hero and nurse, the smashing Rubens hoof
And fist, the witch who rode my bedroom roof
And made my finger bleed, after all are man and wife
Whose mortal ribs I cracked to water my life,
Whose eyes I weighted keeping my late hours,
Loving my boys, chain-smoking in late, dead bars,
Watching the first light pickle Storrow Drive.

Why did I need that empty space to live?
The hand in the dark was my own, God knows whose cars.

The clay gods lean, and cast shadows under the stars,
Enjoying the blameless flowers on their Boston roof.
The watering-can's bland nozzle gleams like a hoof.

To Salter's Point

Frances Wadsworth Valentine
1880–1959

Here in Framingham, black, unlikely
Wheel spoking into mild Republican townships,
I have come to where the world drops off
Into an emptiness that cannot bear
Or lacks the center to compel
The barest sparrow feather's falling.
Maybe our mortal calling
Is, after all, to fall
Regarded by some most tender care:
But here, the air
Has grown too thin: the world drops off
That could imagine Heaven, or so much care.

Framingham is building. The savage ring
And shake of the drill turn up your morphined sleep.
I fall, still in earth's monstrous pull,
To kiss your hands, your planeless face.
Oh, you are right
Not to know your death-bed's place;
To wander in your drugs from Framingham
To Salter's Point, the long blond beaches where
You and your brothers peeled oranges and swam
While your parents looked on in daguerreotype.

Your iron bedstead there was white like this:
And in this grave, unspeakable night,
Beyond the pull of gravity or care,
You have no place: nor we:

You have taken the summer house, the hedge,
The brook, the dog, our air, our ground down with you,
And all the tall gray children can run
Away from home now and walk forever and ever
And come to nothing but this mouthful of earth,
All endings over.

Lines in Dejection

for my sister

Remember how we spread our hair on the sea,
Phosphorous fans, the moon's edge crumbling under
Moving pieces of sky? Ghostly weeds loitered
Like misty Thetis's hair, or some sea-monster's
Ancient whiskers, floating around our knees;
Moony children, we drifted, and no god or monster
Could have seemed foreign then to our globe of water.
Remember
Lying like still shells on the glass water?
The paper moon opened, a Japanese water flower
Drifting free of its shell in the bowl of the sky.

Who poured it out? In twenty years
The bay is still in its place, they are still there,
Walking slowly by the water.
Have they been here, all along? Have we?
Back, back, I strike out from the ancestral stare
And now the bowl's shadow composes what I see:
The weeds cradle me and draw me under, under.

But there they are, on the pitch-black ocean floor,
Hands out, hair floating: everywhere!
Holding us in their charred arms like water.

Sleep Drops Its Nets

Sleep drops its nets for monsters old as the Flood;
You are not you, no more than I am I;
If our dead fathers walk the wall at night
Our hands when we wake up are white on white
Betraying neither wounds nor blood;
The voice is mist that made us cry.

And then day sweeps the castle dry.

Déjà-vu

No, my father here, as You said,
When I asked him for bread
Didn't refuse me; but the bread was green;
And now You!
Now I'm dry and cold,
Chattering in the corner of the greenhouse,
Now You let me know it was always You,
That déjà-vu
Tilt of the sunlight on the floor,
That silence at the door!
I'd laugh, but I never, never loved You,
And here I am dead,
My Midas teeth on edge, green
Jade on jade.

Sunset at Wellfleet

A spit of sky, awash with Venetian gold
Hangs over the Congregational bell-tower, where
Last night the Northern Lights sifted their fire,
Shot through with the airless dark, romantic and cold.
The sun doesn't move, but suddenly is gone,
The cloudy tide goes out, and leaves a ring.
Easy to die: we knew it all along:
Knee-high to the dark as of old:
These words I tell you smoking in my eye:
The tree-frog is the tree-frog. The sky is the sky,
The rattling bay runs night and day *I, I, I,*
Over and over, turning on itself: there,
Where it curls on emptiness: there I sing.

Asleep over Lines from Willa Cather

Now I lay me desolate to sleep
Cold in the sound of the underground flood,
Brushed in half-sleep by the phantom plant
Pressed in the book by my bed
Blue green leaves, large and coarse-toothed . . .
With big white blossoms like Easter lilies . . .
Latour recognized the noxious datura.
In its dead shade I lay me down to sleep.

The reins inside my head that hold my hope
When it leaps, in waking life, fall slack,
And, beyond the world of falling things,
With flesh like air, and an assumed agreement
Between my body and the way it takes,
I walk aimlessly by a green and perfect river.

The garden is here, as I knew it would be;
The garden imagined through oblique windows in paintings,

Earth's lost plantation, waiting for all, all,
All to be well: the fountain translates the sun.
I do not see but know God follows me,
And I follow, without fear of madness,
Paths and turnings that are both wild and formal,
Of all colors or none, tiger-lily and rock,
Pools dead with the weight of fallen leaves, and falls,
Follow after him I love, who waits in the garden.

Mercy, Pity, Fear and Shame
Spring in this garden, for it is earth's.
My body is not air, it casts a shadow.
At the next turning I come upon him I love
Waiting by the tree from my childhood that drops
White petals that hugely snow on the whitening ground.
He takes my arm and we walk a little way
Away from the tree towards the shining river
Running clear green through the garden.

The allegorists' arrow has struck me down.
I freeze in the noise of the flood.
When my love bends to speak, it is a language
I do not know: I answer and have no voice,
I am deaf, I am blind, I reach out to touch his face
And touch a spot of spittled clay, my eye,
Hiding the garden, the river, the tree.

Cambridge by Night

Down the aisles of this dark town
Pass faces and faces I have known
In the green, dog days, I forget their names,
Forget their faces.

Every public place in this city
Is a sideshow of souls sword-swallowing pity:

Father Dog-face barks without a sound,
The penny candles stare me down.

You were so close I could have touched the dead
Childhood in your face,
Left my mother's house a bride
With a light,
Night-light, dawn, to be by your side
All night,
But wanting pity, pity stood
Between us in your face.

Nothing troubles the dark: the last
Tiffany windows are out. Their ghosts
Might be my dutch uncles; pity
it's summer, they're out of the city.

To a Friend

I cannot give you much or ask you much.
Though I shore myself up until we meet,
The words we say are public as the street:
Your body is walled up against my touch.

Our ghosts bob and hug in the air where we meet,
My reason hinges on arcs you draw complete,
And yet you are walled up against my touch.

Your love for me is, in its way, complete,
Like alabaster apples angels eat,
But since it is in this world that we meet
I cannot give you much or ask you much.

You go your way, I mine, and when we meet,
Both half-distracted by the smells of the street,
Your body is walled up against my touch.

My body sings at your table, waits on the street
And you pass empty-handed, till when we meet
I have been so far, so deep, so cold, so much,
My hands, my eyes, my tongue are like bark to the touch.

Waiting

Ask, and let your words diminish your asking,
As your journal has diminished your days,
With the next day's vanity drying your blood,
The words you have lost in your notebooks.
Ask—do not be afraid. Praise Him for His silence.

What I love to ask is what I know,
Old thoughts that fit like a boot.
What I would hazard clings in my skull:
Pride intervenes, like an eyelid.

All sound slows down to a monstrous slow repetition,
Your times of reflection become a dark shop-window,
Your face up against your face.
You kneel, you see yourself see yourself kneel,
Revile your own looking down at your looking up;
Before the words form in the back of your head
You have said them over and answered, lives before.
O saints, more rollicking sunbeams, more birds about your heads!
Catherine, more Catherine-wheels!

Sic transit gloria mundi,
The quick flax, the swollen globe of water.
Sic transit John's coronation, mortal in celluloid.
Underground roots and wires burn under us.
John outlives the Journal's 4-color outsize portrait
Suitable for Framing, flapping, no color,
No love, in the rain on the side of the paper-shed.

Into Thy hands, O Lord, I commit my soul.
All Venice is sinking.

Let us dance on the head of a pin
And praise principalities!

Life is a joke and all things show it!
Let us praise the night sounds in Connecticut,
The Czechoslovak's parakeet,
Whistling *Idiot, Idiot!*

The moon's disk singes a bucketing cloud
Lit by the sun lit by a burning sword
Pointing us out of the Garden.

Turn your back on the dark reflecting glass
Fogged up with the breath of old words:

You will not be forgiven if you ignore
The pillar of slow insistent snow
Framing the angel at the door,
Who will not speak and will not go,

Numbering our hairs, our bright blue feathers.

Sasha and the Poet

Sasha: I dreamed you and he
Sat under a tree being interviewed
By some invisible personage. You were saying
'They sound strange because they were lonely,
The seventeenth century,
That's why the poets sound strange today:
In the hope of some strange answer.'

Then you sang '*hey nonny, nonny, no*' and cried,
And asked him to finish. '*Quoth the potato-bug,*'
He said, and stood up slowly.
'By Shakespeare.' And walked away.

The Second Dream

We all heard the alarm. The planes were out
And coming, from a friendly country. You, I thought,
Would know what to do. But you said,
'There is nothing to do. Last time
The bodies were like charred trees.'

We had so many minutes. The leaves
Over the street left the light silver as dimes.
The children hung around in slow motion, loud,
Liquid as butterflies, with nothing to do.

A Bride's Hours

I. DAWN
I try to hold your face in my mind's million eyes
But nothing hangs together. My spirit lies
Around my will like an extra skin
I cannot fill or shake.
My eyes in Bachrach's rectangle look in.
I, who was once at the core of the world,
Whose childish outline held like a written word,
Am frozen in blur: my body, waiting, pours
Over its centaur dreams, and drowns, and wakes
To terror of man and horse.

2. THE BATH

My sisters walk around touching things, or loll
On the bed with last month's *New Yorker*s. My skin,
Beaded with bath-oil, gleams like a hot-house fake:
My body holds me like an empty bowl.
It is three, it is four, it is time to come in
From thinking about the cake to eat the cake.
My sisters' voices whir like cardboard birds
On sticks: married, they flutter and wheel to find
In this misted looking-glass their own lost words,
In the exhaled smoke.
                              There isn't a sound,
Even the shadows compose like waiting wings.
I am the hollow circle closed by the ring.

3. NIGHT

I am thrown open like a child's damp hand
In sleep. You turn your back in sleep, unmanned.
How can I be so light, at the core of things?
My way was long and crooked to your hand!
What could your jeweled glove command
But flight of my stone wings?
Our honeymoon lake, ignoring the lit-up land,
Shows blank Orion where to dip his hand.

Afterbirth

I loiter in the eye of the Slough,
Every joint aching for sleep;
The sky, inhumanly deep,
Sarcastically casts back the Slough.

Did my child take breath to cry
At the slick hand that hooked her out,

Or cry to breathe? or did she lie
Still in her private dark, curled taut

Under her sleep's hobgoblin shout?
Anesthesia blew me out:
I gardened shadows in my lost crib
While they took her from me like a rib.

Swaddled and barred, she curls in sleep
At the dry edge of mortality.
If the sky's side proves too steep
Who will take up the little old lady,

Who will call her by her name
When she's a crumble of bones?
What logos lights the filament of time,
Carbon arc fusing birth-stone to head-stone?

The mud pulls harder: the stepping stones
Shake in front of my swimming eyes.
There dear, there dear, here's a pill:
Sleep, sleep, all will be well:
Lull-lullaby.

Sarah's Christening Day

Our Lord, today is Sarah's christening day.
I wouldn't build the child a house of straw,
Teach her to wait and welcome the holy face
With candles of prayer, or pray, if the wager were all.
But I have never seen or loved the holy face.
I don't believe the half of what I pray.

This world is straw: straw mother, father, friend,
Per omnia saecula saeculorum, amen.
But Lord! it shines, it shines, like light, today.

Tired of London

When you came to town,
Warm bubbling rains came, the teething leaves,
Steaming spring earth, and the tough, small-footed birds;

Reckless colors sifted the closed, dense sky
As we went hand in hand through our larky maze
In the cultivated stubble of Hampstead Heath:

Monkshood, Foxglove, Canterbury Bells
Composed themselves to drink the bovril air
Thinned by the watery sun.

You, with no sense of giving,
Brought all the dangers I no longer dared;
Netted the wind that roared through my rented bed,

And, poised like Eros over Picadilly,
Were always there.
I cannot find the words to leave you with.

This way love's conversation, the body and mind of it, goes
On after love: we shall come to call this love,
And this roar in our ears which before very long
We become, we shall call our song.

Cambridge
April 27, 1957

Your letter made me see myself grown old
With only the past's poor wing-dust shadows to hold,
Dressed in violet hand-me-downs, half-asleep, only half,
Queer as nines in the violet dust of my mind,
Leaning in some sloping attic, like this one where I write

You all night,
The wet, metaphorical Cambridge wind
Sorry on the skylight.
                              The New England landscape goes
Like money: but here on Agassiz Walk we save
Everything we have
Under Great-Aunt Georgie's georgian bed;
A knot garden roots through Great-Aunt Georgie's toes
Three floors below: when summer comes, God knows
We'll dry the herbs Aunt Georgie grows:
Who knows, who knows
What goes on in her head.

I read Thoreau myself, I listen for Thoreau
Up here; wonder if there's a burial mound
Anywhere for Henry: PAX, AETAT.
45. Quiet Desperation. REQUIESCAT,

Ducky: one of these nice days
My niece, the one with one glass eye,
Is driving me out to Walden Pond:
Cross my heart, I hope to die.

New York
April 27, 1962

When we get old, they say, we'll remember
Things that had sunk below the mind's waking reach
In our distracted years; someday, knees blanketed, I will reach out
To touch your face, your brown hair.

Remember now thy Creator in the days of thy youth.
I rest, tending children, in hollow, light rooms,
Sleep in their milky fingers, after years
Howling up on the tiles while my goblins threw their shoes.

The child I carry lies alone:
Which hag did we not invite to its conception?
I cat-nap, remembering the tiles.

And you?
Steps on the sidewalk outside my barred New York windows
Land on the cracks, let out the bears,
Loose them on the child who is not there;
Footsteps that gleam in their echo of SS men's heels
Off-stage in my first movies: approaching the door.
We huddle inside and wake to remember it's Peace.
Peace. But you are not here, nor are you dead.

No-one forgot my birthday. Twenty-eight.
How shall we celebrate?
Fetch my blanket, dearest, there's something in the air,
Dark, quick, quicksilver, dark eyes, brown hair,
Bringing all the presents: someone is coming late:
The babies cry, the bell rings in thin air.

September 1963

We've been at home four years, in a kind of peace,
A kind of kingdom: brushing our yellow hair
At the tower's small window,
Playing hop-scotch on the grass.

With twenty other Gullivers
I hover at the door,
Watch you shy through this riddle of primary colors,
The howling razzle-dazzle of your peers.

Tears, stay with me, stay with me, tears.
Dearest, go: this is what

School is, what the world is.
Have I sewed my hands to yours?

Five minutes later in the eye of God
You and Kate and Jeremy are dancing.

Glad, derelict, I find a park bench, read
Birmingham. Birmingham. Birmingham.
White tears on a white ground,
White world going on, white hand in hand,
World without end.

Riverside

Now, with March forcing our brittle spines like first childbirth,
Scattering our notes, making the house cold inside,
Riverside Park turns up its vestiges of God
Where bare-faced boys in their sweat-suits lope through the last light
Alongside long-haired girls, half-tree,
And every dog is a brother, or half-brother,
And the cold-war babies span their tender fists,
198?, to net the sun
Spun gold in these thousand pigeon brown windows
Then OUT in a mushroom of neon over Hoboken:
And I, like you, am I, in the eyes of the angels.

Winter was the time for the kind of death we enjoyed:
Then the crust of the earth was something arbitrary;
Branches roots, the sky a vein of tin,
Leaves rose, smoke fell, all the old ladies
Waiting on the benches grew beards waiting.
We talked on the phone, napped, grew white and dry
And leapt at misunderstanding, forcing the news
Every day, the news of the end of love

From the earth's four corners: then left home in the dark,
Dropping pebbles behind us, came
Into the cold: tears from the cold
Stood in our eyes like tears.

Now, with March,
The woods begin to move, and I
Hold your body in my mind, and see
In each man here a mooning orphan boy,
In every long-haired girl a bearded lady,
In every dog the green part of my mind.
That couple stops: tenderly
He carves their initials in her bright green bark.
She takes a child, the moon climbs one slow step
And stands alone; and I
Keep in and chip in my sleep at winter's bone.

For Teed

April 6th: the country thaws and drips,
The worm turns under the town,
Under the world: the freed earth gapes
In wily Ulysses' lips,
The dust of his wrist rests
In caves that were Penelope's breasts,
Even the dog is gone
White-eyed to Acheron:
No Elizabeth, no Jack
Has come back.
Here lies Teed.
Surviving her are

God, can you hear her
Sing? how earth is freed
Of Teed's winter,

Morphine, flowers
Curled on the radiator,
Freed of her visiting hours,
The night sounds of St. Luke's,
Of her fortune-cookie body, freed
Of the whole table reading *cancer*:
The needle trembles, breaks!
Her face swells: can you hear?
Freed of her! of her!

My Grandmother's Watch

Your first child was my father,
Old *muti* of Buffalo, little old child heiress,
My black-eyed baby, chain-smoking gold-
Tipped English Ovals in Heaven: your brassy
Churchillian French reduced us all to *mots*,
Even from the hardly troubled, lavendered sheets of your deathbed.

I wear your coin-thin red gold watch now, Momma,
Its face benign as the Archduke's, and think of your hours,
And what has gone between us, what is ours.
Tonight, for instance: my tongue is thick with longing:
When the children's visit was over, the cake cleared away,
What possessed your mahogany beasts to stay?

On the night of my eighteenth birthday
You made me a toast, saying I
Was not only good at school, but musical!
Pink-cheeked, black-hearted, shy,
I couldn't even look you in the eye:
They cleared the cake away.

The insanely steady minute-hand sweeps round,
The hours go by. Somebody said

His Viennese grandfather
Sold him his watch on his deathbed.
Did you too?

What can I do?

O Momma, what can I
Do with this gold and crystal that goes by?

The Beast with Two Backs

Excursion: a night, two days
Away from home and neighborhood,
Double-locked doors, mirror-
Backed peep-holes: the neighbors.

How big they've grown, the children!
Make them walk! It's not good,
A woman, the insides! Daughters,
You'll always have them; five sons,
One's in Teaneck. Make her walk!
You'll break your mother's back!

The boat: by Christ, an excursion.
Every man has seven wives, each wife
Has seven children, each child has seven guns.
The ladies change, they do change, in the Ladies'
Room: they wink, they shrug, they look over their backs
At their colorful tails. I look at my toes
In the stall where the toilet roils with the white Atlantic.

Over the Times we talk about Ho,
Allen Dulles, Malcolm X: take up our Signet Classics.
Someone across the way from us is reading *The Guermantes' Way*,
Who smiles. It is a long trip to our island,

Seven years already,
Longer than anyone ever would have thought.
We buy beer; I'd like
A colorful tail like that.

On our island we walk, eat, lie,
Drink, walk, analyze, analyze.
This moon we do not like we'll like
Remembering, and know it.
Do we trust ourselves more this morning?
Today we can stay in bed all day. Ah, love,

The soap, Irina! You have no soap! The sheets,
Irina, in Six! Knock knock.

Knock. We give it up, we are married
Seven years, we can smile with the backs of our heads:
The two-backed beast is wild,
We let him go.
                    He said. She said.
He said.
            We turn our backs
For home.
            On the wall it said "For Fire:
Continuous ringing of bell and call of FIRE."

The Little Flower

I thank God, I have never taken to drinking, as many I know have, I
    have never done that and my children should be thankful but they
    are not, I have not been that kind,
I say my prayers every night,
Lots of them do and with less reason, I did once but put it from me,
    and with all the shocks I have had to bear, such shocks in those ter-
    rible years, you do not know, my father, my father was a mean man,

Given to giving nicknames,
He called me Susan B. Anthony because I was so strong I guess, I have
never given way as others would have done, he called your aunt
Bunny because when her first two teeth came in he said *she looks
just like a bunny*, she did look just like a bunny, *we will call her
Bunny* and so she is to this day I am eighty-three she must be
eighty, strange she was always jealous of my looks Bun was, I was
tall and slim
And very beautiful they all said so,
And she thought I had all the looks always was a jealous kind of per-
son but you know she was very lovely too, I was jealous of her too,
isn't that funny I always thought Bun had such nice feet and I al-
ways thought my feet were ugly isn't that funny, the things you will
get into your head, feet
It hasn't all been roses,
My mother was a Ross a Ross from Scotland, they were a noble clan,
your mother sent me a postcard once of the Ross castle, I have it
somewhere in these suitcases, it's in the north
Oh I must set my things in order
I must have help to set my things in order, so many papers, no one
will come and soon I will be gone and then who will, No now we
will talk it is so good, to have someone to talk to, is that chair all
right for you not in a draft, this room has a terrible draft you have
beautiful eyes,
A little like mine oh when I was younger
You have always been a good child and you know you get funny all
alone in a room I hope I have never complained but you get and at
my age, no one understands what it is like to be old, does my mind
wander, that is what I
I forget things
Words do not come to my mind, my mother was a Ross from Scot-
land, they were a noble clan, she used to tell such wonderful stories
and sing us the old songs she would go on with those stories and
songs the children loved her, she came and visited us often and
stayed weeks and weeks, she was always there if I were sick, I hope
she always knew she had a home with us and I was sick so much
with the climate what it was and the miscarriages and the babies,
and she always came to be a comfort to me, but then she died,

What it is like

He had died long before that, there is a place for Bun and a place for
    me with them in the plot in Minneapolis, I don't care about cre-
    mation it seems the cleanest thing you don't mind talking about
    these things do you, neither do I some people do but I don't mind
    talking about these things at all, look at my teeth, if I do not get to
    the dentist, but I cannot even get dressed, just to get dressed but I
    get so dizzy, when I stand I am so afraid of falling again, will you
    look at my teeth, I try not to smile so as to show them, I always
    had beautiful teeth

It seems the cleanest thing

Bunny has written me a long letter about it, she's going to be cre-
    mated, Henry was too, you pack a bag with the clothes you want
    to go in and if you go in winter like her Henry did, and a godsend,
    they wait till Spring to put you in the ground, Henry's there, no I
    don't mind about cremation as long as they make sure I'm good
    and dead first, ha, ha,

Look at my teeth

The children loved her, she would tell them those stories over and
    over, no I don't remember any of them, not one, and the children
    don't any more, I asked Louise and she said, No Mother, I like to
    tell you these things because soon I will be gone and then no one
    will remember all this

My father

There do you hear her, there she goes, eight or ten hours a day some
    days, they say she is an opera singer, it goes right through my
    spine, we would always come to New York here for the opera sea-
    son, we always took the same suite at the Plaza Hotel, the manager
    was a very fine gentleman, he always said to me, Mrs. Haran, your
    children are the best behaved children who have ever visited us
    here at the Plaza Hotel, and they were, so quiet

They all said so

Your grandfather used to love the operas and then we always had sea-
    son tickets for the Chicago Symphony, I would take the children
    every Friday afternoon, do you hear her, I have sent a note to the
    desk but they say there is nothing they can do, I must take another
    room, on another floor, another hotel

Just to get dressed

Your mother always had a gift for music, she had lessons from the age
of five with the best piano teacher in the city, but no when she
married him she let it go, I told her, you will be sorry Louise, if
you have music you will always have that whatever comes, like
books, my children all loved books if you give children the love of
books they will always have that whatever comes, will you listen to
that woman, I have told them at least let her be still Sundays, at
least let me have peace Sundays but you know they are all Jewish
people in this hotel

Not that I

Not that I have anything against Jewish people if you like them I hope
I am not so narrow, it is all knishes, what are they, and lox and the
good Lord knows what on the menu, I cannot eat it, Ramon my
waiter says ¡Ah Mrs. Haran you did not eat! they all loved reading,
if I could only read but it hurts my eyes so

Even the Tribune

With everything else I had to bear there were always books, I used to
read a book a day, oh yes and magazines, Edward used to tease me
for taking the Post but I have always said there are lots of fine arti-
cles in the Post I still take it but now I can hardly read the Tribune,
Dr. Giroux wants me to see an ophthalmologist

Just to get dressed

Edward your uncle Edward was a great reader, he was always reading,
he always said he loved to read with me there in the room, we al-
ways read together like that when he was little, those were bad
years, that was when it was just beginning, he was reading to him-
self at three years, his teachers always told me, Eddie has a wonder-
ful mind, they called him Eddie, I was always with him when he
was little, that was when your grandfather began to take too much,
then I was so ill and Edward would always come in and sit by me,
I was in bed so much, months at a time, Edward would say
Mother shall I sit with you a while, he was always considerate that
way most children are not you know, Edward was

To be a comfort

They were seven brothers the children's uncle Jack was first, the mon-
signor, then your grandfather, and the others were all born over
here, well they scattered around the middle west, mostly farming
and such, your grandfather was the only one of them who ever

made his way, and Jack, one went to California I think, oh the Lord
knows where they all are now living or dead, they all blamed me
Listen to her
We had an audience with the Pope did I ever tell you that I like to tell
you these things, Pope Pius X, he was a very charming man,
charming, a gentleman I shall never forget it, a private audience,
no he spoke English, your uncle Jack was at the American College,
he arranged it all, no I went to the Church long before I ever met
your grandfather I was still at home well it seemed to draw me in I
don't know why, my father said it was just like me, *The Little
Flower* he called me
A religious man, they were all religious men
I have always held that your church doesn't matter as long as you live
right you must give the children some faith to stand by them when
their troubles come, it doesn't matter what church I hope I am not
so narrow, but it breaks my heart to see Billy and her raising those
children without anything, he always went to the best Catholic
schools, I gave him that, and how can he stand by and watch her
raise those children with nothing, and how can she let him get
so heavy
It's the drinking
I'm sorry, I hope I've always been good to her the same as I am with
all of you yet she never brings them, they are my grandchildren
and I never see them, they do not know me, they lose that you
know, they will never have those memories, it is nice to have a
sense of family
They all blamed me
We went down, Jack had a summer place at that castle Gandolfo you
know, very nice, outside Rome, it was hot, I remember I was faint
do you hear her ah-ah-ah-ah, no no coffee for me I can't take it,
my lower intestine, well, and then I get so terribly dizzy, Dr. Giroux
has given me pills for it but I don't like to take them, just some ice
water is all, there in that green bottle, Tipperary was where they
came from but they were originally Normans
Normans who came over from France
Jack was good to us at first, for a while, at the beginning he would
take his dinner with us every night, so as to keep the idea of a fam-
ily for the children, he cared a lot for that, priests do they don't

know, that was when it was beginning with your grandfather, the
stocks dropping and his partner and all and the never coming home
The children never knew
I spared them that, and the miscarriages, it was not so easy in those
days to have a baby, you girls today, and my back was never strong
to carry them, six months in bed before Billy, and then the broth-
ers tried to get me to have him back, they all blamed me
Normans
I was never off a penny in my books when I was spending thousands
of dollars managing Astor Street and now I'm always so confused
that is what terrifies me, my checkbook is in such a state and no
one, I ask Billy but he never comes, I guess she won't let him away,
I don't think much of a person like that, I like to keep two thou-
sand dollars margin in case I have to go to the hospital or so when
I go it will, but it's under that now I don't know how much and I
make mistakes in my arithmetic, and then these medicines, forty
dollars, fifty dollars, I feel awful, the children do not understand or
they would not be so
What it is like
None of you, but you are a good child, I always had a special place in
my heart even when you were little, of course I loved you all, and I
worry so about you, when you get old you worry a lot, there's some
nice cake in there on the shelf chocolate the kind you like, I got it
in last week expecting you, oh I know how much you have to do at
home, I hope you're through having children now, two is a nice
family plenty these days, you know just a phone call would mean a
lot when you have a minute
The children do not know
I hate to call you I know how busy you are, I hope I haven't asked
much of my family, I know you're all caught up in your own life
the family and all, you look tired, I loved my children I hope I
loved my children
None of you
I hope I was good to him, everything a wife should be, he was proud
of me, all my clothes were made specially for me, and I was never
off a penny in my books and they all loved to come to Astor Street,
I remember Mr. Fairbank a millionaire there, he used to always
come and he could have had anything in the world, he loved to
come to us, he said, Nelly I feel at home here, a charming man, a

very old family, no airs, no I never turned him away while he was well, I was everything a wife should be, it wasn't easy but men are that way and I hope I never let him know while he was well
Anything in the world
He used to say, Nelly, you make me feel very grateful, and he tried to be very considerate that way while he was well, not all men do, you know, he did try
Music whatever comes
What could I do, it was such a shock, the money, and then him never coming home and the drinking, I had the children to think of, they never knew, Jack tried to help him, first talking himself then the doctors, but nothing helped, he got worse, worse, he had had so much, risen from nothing himself, and he became deluded after the drop, losing more and more, he was on the telephone talking business as if he were still what he had been, then I had to call back, I was so ashamed, and explain he was not well, everyone was very kind, I couldn't go out of the house
I had the children to think of
I kept everything just as it had been for them, Dr. Lapham their doctor, he was a world-famous pediatrician, he died of pneumonia in Boston, he had called on me the day before he went just to see how we were getting along, he said, Mrs. Haran try to do for the children just as you would have done, and I did, Billy went to Canterbury and Harvard, Louise had a beautiful debut, I always had all her clothes made specially for her and there wasn't a better dressed girl her year, or a prettier, it wasn't as if we had a lot
Dr. Lapham
But I always remembered what Dr. Lapham had said, many women would not have done it that way for their children, I should have thought of my own old age
Dr. Lapham
They all blamed me when he was put in the mental home, it was the best state institution in the middle west, I had the children to think of, they said there was money enough for private care but I knew what there was and I knew he couldn't be helped, we had spoken to the best doctors in Chicago, do you know what the private places cost, and he lived, he lived for years and years, he only died three years ago, there wasn't that kind of money for him, look how I've had to manage all these years, and I had to do for the

children it would all have gone, what would I have done, no he
hadn't lost much yet but he would have if he'd gone on, I had to
save what I could
I knew
They kept trying to get him away, one Christmas they got him out, a
trick, and brought him down to Minneapolis, it was Christmas
night, so cold, and we had to take him back, he was not respon-
sible then for what he said, he was ill the doctors could not do any-
thing for him, the money was gone, all but what I had managed to
keep away, I had the children to think of, and myself
He was not responsible then
Then later Billy and your mother brought him east to another state
home, New York State, up here, they said it was a better place, no
they never visited him, he did not know them anymore they said,
that was when they were grown of course when they were young
they never knew
They all blamed me
Dr. Lapham did not blame me, I asked him, in the worst of it, I had
no one to turn to and I asked him and he said, it is very hard
Mrs. Haran, he understood and Edward understood he was older
than the others and I used to talk to him I had no one, oh of
course I didn't tell him the truth, but he was with me and that was
a comfort, Bun came but she did not understand ever, she always
thought he could be helped by the doctors, she never understood
They all blamed me
We didn't see her for a long while and then we didn't talk about it any
more, but I knew she blamed me, she used to say, he loves you
Nelly, she never understood he had never loved me never, only the
house and the clothes and that
Edward understood
He was always with me if it hadn't been for Edward there were times I
would have committed suicide, I know it's a terrible thing to say,
but those were terrible years, but for Edward who always under-
stood, and he was always there, later I wanted him to go out and
get a place of his own, make his life away from all my troubles, but
he always said No Mother and he always stayed until he died four
years ago, the night he died his car went over a bridge
It was the eye drops

He'd been reading Stendahl On Love, he was always a great reader,
    when he died the doctor came in the middle of the night and gave
    me an injection, she was so kind to me that country doctor, she
    understood
Edward understood
It is a terrible thing to lose a child, no matter how old they are they are
    always your children and you always worry, I gave them every-
    thing, and then he died, and the other two never come, what have
    I done, your mother came when he died to be with me, she
    blamed me, I know she blamed me
Never only the house
She did not know how it was with Edward, the drinking and the
    trouble, I never told anyone, he needed me, thank God I had the
    money to help him out of his trouble, it was always the same, I
    was always there
Died, died
I should have thought more of myself, other women would have saved
    for themselves, learn from your grandmother
Christmas night
What it is like to be old, and alone, and sick, and I worry so about
    money, not about leaving a lot behind, I have done enough I hope,
    but I don't know how long I'll last, which will go first, ha, ha, the
    money or me
Always the same
Every night when I lie down I think they'll find me in the morning, I
    always have the bag ready, that blue one dear you should know,
    every night I wash my feet before I get into bed, they never think
    what it is like,
The children loved her,
Thousands of dollars, I loved my children, I hope I loved my children,
    what have I done that they are strangers to me, sometimes at night
    when I can't sleep
Whatever comes
I never sleep till three or four in the morning or five and then at eight
    or nine she starts up with her scales sometimes I think I must have
    said something or done something to hurt them, something I do
    not know, do you know? then I pray
Deliver her soul, O Lord

And that has been a comfort to me these last years, though what the
   Lord has done for me I don't know, I hope I've always lived right,
   and surely the Lord should not refuse His creatures
And let my cry come unto Thee
Most children are not you know, Edward was, they all blamed me,
   always the same, gone, and then no one, look at my teeth, I am
   afraid to die, you are young but you know you get afraid
I knew
It's good to talk like this to someone, and then I like to tell you these
   things, never, only the house, died, died, died, soon I will be gone
   and then no one will remember, there do you hear her, none of you.

   Sex

All the years waiting, the whole, barren, young
Life long. The gummy yearning
All night long for the far white oval
Moving on the ceiling;
The hand on the head, the hand in hand;
The gummy pages of dirty books by flashlight,
Blank as those damaged classical groins;

Diffusion of leaves on the night sky,
The queer, sublunar walks.
And the words: the lily, the flame, the truelove knot,
Forget-me-not; coming, going,
Having, taking, lying with,
Knowing, dying;
The old king's polar sword,
The wine glass shattered on the stone floor.

And the thing itself not the thing itself,
But a metaphor.

Adam and Eve: Poem on Folded Paper

We dream of saving what
cannot
Can't touch through this glass
pane
Pain that cuts the green world
down
Down, derry down with my true
love
Loving the one human voice we
heard
Heard myself answer in a
dream
Dream now, Adam, and wake to find no
world
The world's a dance of spiders against this
pane
And pain is their condition.

Dream Barker

We met for supper in your flat-bottomed boat.
I got there first: in a white dress: I remember
Wondering if you'd come. Then you shot over the bank,
A Virgilian Nigger Jim, and poled us off
To a little sea-food barker's cave you knew.

What'll you have? you said. Eels hung down,
Bamboozled claws hung up from the crackling weeds.
The light was all behind us. To one side
In a dish of ice was a shell shaped like a sand-dollar
But worked with Byzantine blue and gold. *What's that?*

Well, I've never seen it before, you said,
And I don't know how it tastes.
Oh well, said I, *if it's bad,*
I'm not too hungry, are you? We'd have the shell . . .
I know just how you feel, you said

And asked for it; we held out our hands.
Six Dollars! barked the barker, *For This Beauty!*
We fell down laughing in your flat-bottomed boat,

And then I woke up: in a white dress:
Dry as a bone on dry land, Jim,
Bone dry, old, in a dry land, Jim, my Jim.

To My Soul

after Hadrian and Ronsard

Scattered milkweed, valentine,
Moonlighting darling, leonine
Host and guest of my chêateau,

Tender, yawning concubine,
Vine of my summer in decline,
Uncut, unribboned mistletoe,

Monstrous footprint in the snow,
Hypnotizing, gemmy toad,
My generations' cameo,

Symplegadês of every road,
Closet bones, unflowered sod,
Laugh, my little nuncio!

Pilgrims

(1969)

"... but I say whatever
one loves, is"
                        —Sappho

Part I

The Couples

One night they all
found themselves alone,
their first force gone.
No law.

Vacations were no vacation,
nothing came in the mail,
and so on. Everyone
wanted to be good,

no one alive remembered them.

Out of decency no one spoke.
By the time day broke
even the babies were bored with them,
with hunger, and falling;

even you, Prince, gray
around the mouth and tired of calling,
tired of briars, tired of them,
had ridden away.

Fireside

The fox went under the garden
thinking. The watersnake
never moved, or the sun.
—Night, and everyone's straight out

longing; the cat's in the woods,
the children lie loose in stories

tall as this world could
be if we could run for it Lord

Fox. Foxfire will, we thought, out,
you and I, blue glass at the fire-
side side by side,
word for word,
wood for wood,
desire for desire,
nicer than God.

Solomon

Still, gold, open-handed,
sad King Solomon
listened: they started,
weightless, close to his ear,
sweet as bees.

One with light breasts and knees
danced with herself before Solomon,
one stood by with barbarian eyes
mad for Solomon,
one, a child, even touched his face

and he smiled in his clothes,
shut his eyes.

Solomon sat by a white pond
his skin thin gold
and his head down.

One stood by with barbarian eyes
mad for Solomon.
She came to his hands,

light, far, anyone
or no one. Solomon
touched her eyes.

                    Too close,
too heavy, the dark
did just what it had promised,

the park turned sharp as it had started:

he closed his hands.

In the Museum

There is a stone
where the Buddha was.
Nothing: air,

one footprint; his chair
a stone.
We stood

back, out of harm;
smiled; right?
went on.

The next room, love,
was funnier: all that love-making
in broad daylight,

and every one of them smiling.
Back where the Buddha was, the stone,
happy as God,

grinned like bone,
love: the air,

asking nothing,

smiled everywhere.

Come.

By the Boat Pond

The newspapers blowing over the street
made her cry, all the birds in New York were crying
because they couldn't speak Greek,

she took nothing with her and went out onto the street.
The day was obscure, one more
lick of the quiet
licking at the door,

her soft black magic,
swallowing him, the children,
the world: leaving, everyone leaving,
all turning angels or nothing,

nothing or swimming like paradise children.

The Summer House

I
She took his hand
so he brought her to his country:
'See it is dry': and

it was a light field, water,
a tree loud as water
in that wind.

—In your country
there is a light field, water.

Your body is in this wind,
I am in your mouth, your hand.

II
There were times
out of time's drag
we'd be without fixed faces
bodies or words; times

held like a feathery scene
on a Quimper plate: v's of quick birds
in their aviary sky, blue flowers
strung all around the dot-faced boy and girl:

all afternoon the sunlight ticked across
sleep, across our borrowed house.

III
The angels we made in the snow
are blown and the shapes at the snow's edge
are only themselves again

and we our taller selves
smoke between the house and the woods' edge,
dying to come in or have snow:

—Does he love her? She loves,
he loves, they

love the old stories of the snow
and the look of the house. Together so.

Woods

Dearest darling woodenhead
I love you

I can taste you
in bed laughing

come on Teach I love your
hair

Penseroso,
crab, you angel!

feel me on the palm of your hand?

Look

all the thin trees
are hanging this morning ready to fuzz,

high birds I can't see are whistling,
winter's dripping down

faster and faster and
faster. And not to death.

Wait.

Her dream: the child

It stared and stared
right through them to the world.

But it better come in said
a quiet man and she said Look
and took it into bed.

They lay closer
in the pale morning. Three flat white ducks
on the wall woke up and took off.

In the morning
he woke them up humming.

Orpheus and Eurydice

'What we spent, we had.
What we had, we have.
What we lost, we leave.'
—Epitaph for his wife and himself,
   by the Duke of Devon, twelfth century

I
You. You running across the field.

A hissing second, not a word,
and there it was, our underworld:
behind your face another, and another,
and I

away.

—And you alive: staring,
almost smiling;

hearing them come down, tearing
air from air.

11

'This dark is everywhere'
we said, and called it light,
coming to ourselves.

                              Fear
has at me, dearest. Even this night
drags down. The moon's gone. Someone
shakes an old black camera-cloth
in front of our eyes.
Yours glint like a snowman's eyes.
We just look on, at each other.

What we had, we have. They circle down.
You draw them down like flies.
You laugh, we run
over a red field, turning at the end to blue air, —
you turning, turning again! the river
tossing a shoe up, a handful of hair.

Goodbye

After Bella Akhmadulina

And finally I'll say goodbye.
Don't feel you have to love.
I'm chattering, crazy,
or maybe coming into a crazier kind of peace.

How you loved! Your lips just grazing over disaster,
tasting nothing. But that doesn't matter.
How you loved! How you destroyed!
Offhandedly, like a great pale curious boy.

O coldness of failure, cold certainty,
there's no settling with you. The body
wanders around, sees light; sun and moon
shine through the glass pane.

The empty body goes on with its little task.
But the hands fall light and slack,
and like a small flock, sideways,
all sounds and smells graze off away.

Separation

I
OK my child
but not unmake
the smudge of black
under his eyes, their eyes,

or turn it back to the quiet, best
time we sat
in the front room; dumb,
dressed, affectionate.

II
There is fear there, but you know
it's fear. Why,
summer's just going to be starting;
I have work,
I have friends,
I have whatever I had.

I mean to take hold
like a tree. There's tar,
bolts, wires. Leaves.

The trees rattle all around.
Jack and Elizabeth live in a hidden house
and hold hands in it;

they smile at me as if in the past,
as if kindly. O Jack and Elizabeth will you marry
marry you will Elizabeth and Jack o. Jack is

rubbing her back
down in front of the summer fire
her eyes are apple green.

Out of the blue, your face
bent over some book you love.

To bed. Sheet lightning on sheet glass, a morning
enough. Enough
I don't understand:

these wires. The white
wet root here
now. These people's bread.

III
The children make spy-maps of the neighbors for you
and paste leaves on. The river wind blows the leaves,
the neighbors rock on cinders hour to hour,
hot. I watch nights from my sliding corner
out to where you are: the street, where your
back goes walking, talking,
talking. You take daylight,
and the law, the way things tick.
And us, wherever you go,—leaves,
how we float, and stick!

IV
Breaking. I just sit. Well,
I hear noises.

I hope to hear noises, wishes
lip up over the steps all night:

flying fish,
my own breathing.

Without knowing anything,
without money, America,
without leaving,

coming to a new country.
Your two hands,
a few names.

Over and over without a smile
the little walls break up and bleed
pure violence and mend and mend.

Thinking about Cain

God to Cain: 'and if thou doest not well,
sin lieth at the door. And unto thee shall be
his desire, and thou shalt rule over him.'

The first life's blood. Now day
lies at the door, the clocks tick,
the smoky kitten nurses at my salty fingers,
not the best. Six-thirty, time

to get up, to get the children up,
to find the mother,
the father.
In the holes they left. Doors!

Ways open to befriend our friends,
our words, our worst old ways, to learn

to love this circling through and through
the veins of those two that day, *thou*.

Dearest,

            this day broke
at ten degrees. I swim
in bed over some dream sentence lost
at a child's crying: the giant on her wall
tips the room over, back:
I tell her all I know,
the walls will settle, he'll go.

Holding her fingers, I watch the sky rise, white.
The frost makes about the same lines
on the same window as last winter,
quicker, quieter . . . I think how nothing's happened,

how to know
to touch a face to make a line
to break the ice to come in time
into this world, unlikely, small,
bloody, shiny, is all, is God's good will
I think, I turn to you,
and fail, and turn,

as the day widens
and we don't know what to do.

Part II

April

Suppose we are standing together a minute
on the wire floor of a *gaswagen*:
suppose we are in the dark.

It's warm and dry.
We have food.
We aren't in hiding waiting, mostly
we're sitting in our own light rooms.

Come over, bring things: bring
milk, peanut butter,
your pills, your woolens, crayons.

Nuns pray.
Snow. It's dark.
Pray for our friends who died
last year and the year
before and who will die this year.

Let's speak,
as the bees do.

Broken-down Girl

Imagine her quick
who could talk
and cry, still
running, under
the whole sky,
the youngest sister,

who fumbled down
in such sincere pieces.
Silver pieces!
The wind,
the Virginia rain,
touch your face

now none of us
at this table
could, frail
gleam, glass face
without a back,
open book,
telstar.

Bin Dream, West Cottage East, D-11

You or I,

sweet Mag, miserable sixteen, paternal,
put the kettle on,
set out three white cups,
and forgot,

the minister edged up sideways
with a certain amount of floor to cross
to the silver sink the radio
the fireplace and the cup,

the sky inched into blue-white milk,
the housemother stood up,
looking at us all, not warmly,
said, *No one*

ate, Mag
put the kettle on

you, your father, your married sister,
or I

Bin Dream #2, Interview with Stravinsky

"Gossip is travel,
and in these times, like travel,
speeded up to the nth degree,
and that's alright,

if you remember of an afternoon
the immeasurable sift
of geological time, the slowness
of say slow snow,

           gossip deriving
from the ancient Aramaic
word, *sari*, or *safari*,

meaning
to travel,
or, to love."

Death House

It was the same kind of night, the light, the coughing,
huge shoes walking, your breathing
through three walls, sleeping into the last things.

In the corner of our grove
the newest one kept on saying
oh, I, oh, I,
Oh him, the guard grinned, going by,
and woke you up. You went ahead.

The guard went ahead.
This is the room, here come the City's dead,
grave sisters, fur-trapping fathers,
mothers still waiting, falling
past my free hands,
and my hands falling.

Archangel

It's dark in here,
your halo looks flat as a plate.
Maybe we're still there. Was that lightning?

You look like a cat when you sleep.
I'm not sleeping. You reading?
I'm looking for this poem,

about a cat—wait a minute—
Go on.
You can read to me all you want.

That time it was lightning.
Is it you? Rolling the green grass back?
I love it when you smile like that.

Is this the white dawn, Angel, in the book?
It's dawn. Look.
Where are they bringing the rock back?

Where are you going?

Half an Hour

Hurt, hurtful, snake-charmed,
struck white together half an hour we tear
through the half-dark after

some sweet core,
under, over gravity,
some white shore . . .

spin, hidden one, *spin*,
trusted to me! laugh sore tooth
sucked warm, sweet; sweet wine

running cool through new
dry shrewd turnings of my soul,
opening veins.

Gull-feathers beating,
beating! Gliding. Still,
sidelong eye . . . wings beating

like words against my eyes.
And your eyes—
o brother-animal, mild,

terrible!—your eyes wait, have been waiting,
knowing,
unknowable, on that sky shore.

A life is waiting.
Its webbed hand
reached out. . .

Trust me!
truth-
telling fish of the sky!

your hand beyond my hand,
your phosphorous trail
broken, lost.

Visiting Day at School

*'She knows she can rub some of her
brown skin off and use it for coloring.'*
—A mother, to Robert Coles

The tall, good, raw-boned, wrong
teacher teaches wrong
glory the children shuffle back from dumb

as we do, too,
having got the problem
right:

what you hold
in your hand
is your hand:

You shall all have prizes, and the last,
they say, first: to come home free,
warm and bare, to laugh to see, Jack,

see the years run
around the tree
to melt to feed you,

Jane, see the line the days flew,
quick bird, down around the thumb,
almost straight,

through all the king's gold,
back.

The Child Jung

'What will become of the boy?'
—his father

"This stone is,
was for ages,
and will be: knows I know,

and it's good, hidden,
hidden I'm a great old doctor, whirling,

an eighteenth-century man whirling
through the woods in a light green carriage,

buckles on my shoes . . . Schoolboy!
the filthiest boy ever made,

or blessed . . . oh curled black
shivering freak!
O my stone God quicksand Eternity!"

Coltrane, Syeeda's Song Flute

*'When I came across it on the piano it reminded
me of her, because it sounded like a happy,
child's song.'*
—Coltrane

To Marilyn, to Peter,
playing, making things: the walls, the stairs,
the attics, bright nests in nests;
the slow, light, grave unstitching of lies,
opening, stinking, letting in air

you bear yourselves in, become your own mother and father,
your own child.
You lying closer.

You going along. Days.
The strobe-lit wheel stops dead
once, twice in a life: old-fashioned rays:

and then all the rest of the time pulls blur,
only you remember it more, playing.

Listening here in the late quiet you can think
great things of us all, I think we will all, Coltrane,
meet speechless and easy in Heaven, our names
known and forgotten, all dearest, all come giant-stepping
out into some wide, light, merciful mind . . .

John
Coltrane, 40, gone
right through the floorboards,
up to the shins, up to the eyes,
closed over,

Syeeda's happy, child's song
left up here, playing.

Photograph of Delmore Schwartz

A young king,
oak, painted and gilded, writing

no one should be so unhappy,
holding his hands out,

but his arms are missing from the shoulders down,
his right side's gone, his mouth's

flaking like a mirror, still
photograph of your childhood,

your son. No one
should be so unhappy, should lie

still in that bending room
where all the atoms fly

off their hooks, animals and children
and friends kill, it was a delusion,

we were not living, the hotel floor
wasn't coming and going and coming

at that great head hurled radiant, flat
at the new world.

The Torn-down Building

Slowly, slowly our exploding time
gives off its lives: a lens, an eyelash rub
under the new ground broken,
under the new primary-colored paint
put up for someone to come to
to start off from to cherish

but dear one this December
the walls walk off, we sit mother-naked
smiling on our boxes of books:
slowly the first snowfall

curls around its own faint fall
each dot different we thought we could
turn back and back to learn, with all this
light everywhere.

The snow falls around as we walk talking war,
books, the times, our friends' funny business.
Lens, eyelash whisper against the flat
stairs outlined in old paint on the open air:
the light draws a thousand thousand window sills,
bottles, our shadows on the floor,
all backs, our piles of books, our toys,
our boxes of letters. Slowly over the newspaper
this quarter century takes in
its infant deaths, gives off its smiling *kouroi*
and we will meet their eyes in the air

    The January light's stock still
a second from your face to mine, mine to the child's,
her words a flare, a fountain lighter than air.

Moon Man

'Here too we dare to hope.'
—Romano Guardini

Swimming down to us
light years
not always a straight line
that was his joke, his night
fears, his pilgrim's climb.

About half way
throwing his silver

suit away he
sees the green earth
click for the first time:

the lightest girl
the heaviest ocean
coming to themselves
and to his hand.

He sets a comradely couple walking
down his white road,
hospitable; hears a shiny
boy and girl, bird and bird
having a time

in his green water.
Clean against it all
one last hour
all alone the moon man's
open everywhere:

This mass is his salt
his girl
        his sky
his work
        his floor.

The Child and the Terrorist, The Terrorist and the Child

The globe's on fire in his hands
and everyone's asleep.

What will we feed him when he comes?
Just getting to know his step, his voice,

my step, a way back in the dark
to where I go without telling lies

or leaving anyone, will take a lifetime,
and it's going slowly,

                              and there's that blue-
white shell I turned my back on at my back,

cracked, stuck to me bone by bone,
turning to stone, wanting to drop,
wanting to turn in a cool globe,
wanting to call

—You, how is it with you?
Archaically cut off. Antarctic miles.

Night

From this night on God let me eat
like that blind child on the train
touching her yogurt as I'd touch a spiderweb
the first morning in the country—sky red—

holding the carton and spoon to her mouth
with all her eyeless body, and then
orientally resting, the whole time smiling
a little to one side of straight ahead.

Pilgrims

Standing there they began to grow skins
dappled as trees, alone in the flare

of their own selves: the fire
died down in the open ground

and they made a place for themselves.
It wasn't much good,
they'd fall, and freeze,

some of them said
Well, it was all they could,

some said it was beautiful, some days,
the way the little ones took to the water,
and some lay smoking, smoking,

and some burned up for good,
and some waited,
lasting, staring
over each other's merciful shoulders,
listening:
          only high in a sudden January thaw
or safe a second in some unsmiling eyes
they'd known always

whispering
Why are we in this life.

Ordinary Things

(1974)

Chalk lines still mark the floor
just where you stood. Our shoulders touched.
I was afraid. You were just saying
ordinary things.
> —Huub Oosterhuis,
> "Twenty Days' Journey"

Part I

After Elegies

Almost two years now I've been sleeping,
a hand on a table that was in a kitchen.

Five or six times you have come by
the window; as if I'd been on a bus

sleeping through the Northwest, waking up,
seeing old villages pass in your face,

sleeping.
       A doctor and his wife, a doctor too, are in the kitchen
area, wide awake. We notice things
differently: a child's handprint in a clay plate, a geranium, aluminum
balconies rail to rail, the car horns of a wedding,

blurs of children in white. *LIFE* shots
of other children.   Fire to paper; black

faces, judge faces, Asian faces; flat
earth   your face   fern   coal

'Autumn Day'

Who has no house now will not build him one . . .
Will waken, read, and write long letters . . .
—Rilke, 'Autumn Day'

The house in the air is rising, not
settling between any trees.

Its lines may have come here by machine,
wirephoto, they soften to dots in the rain.

What draws you on so hard?
    You would like to think
about resting
a minute on the mobbed walk or
the electrocardiograph table
        to ask about the house there—dark,
        stone, floating out over the edge of the buildings,
        someone, something, it may be, inside—
but you can't stop here: the dangerous air,
the crowds, the lights, the hardening Indian Summer . . .

    strange quiet,
with time for work, your evenings, you will write long letters
this winter, you have your friends,
and the names of friends of friends.

He said,

"When I found where we had crashed, in the snow, the two of us,
alone, I made a plan. It takes all my energy to like it.
The trees keep thinning, and the small animals.
She swims over me every night like warmth, like my whole life
going past my eyes. She is the sleep they talk about, and some days
all I can want is sleep."

Forces

This man, blind and honored,
listens to his student reader;
this man did what he thought

and sickens in jail; another
comes to the end of his work;
another threw himself out.

Us too, our destinies get on,
into middle age.

Today we visited a field of graves—
slaves' or Indians' graves, you said—
sunk, unmarked, green edges of hammered granite
sharp as a shoulder blade.
                                        God break me out
of this stiff life I've made.

Kin

A woman's face at the window,
white, composed, tells me I
do not love her; I did not love him;
I do not love my children, so they wither,
so she will take them, take them away.

I cannot love him: he is dead. And she—
she will not hurt us now.

But the somber child;
and the wind, and the white window.

Anesthesia

Right after her birth they crowded in,
into the white room, huge tall masks
of women's faces

brick-red lips, chalked-in triangular eyes
gazed at us: nothing; said:
nothing; not-women they were suicides, trees, soft,
pale, freckled branches bending over her—
I knew them as my own, their cries
took on the family whiskey voice, refusal,
need,—their human need peeled down, tore,
scratched for her life—
I hacked and hacked them apart—

then who knows
when you murder things like that
who comes in and takes over

After Elegies (2)

The doctors tell me, "Swim.
You are beginning, moving on; yes,
trailing his side, still
amazed at your own body apart; yes, looking back,
you don't have to smile that way, afraid
we are not here; you are beginning,
leaving nothing; your friend is here
with you, and you know him,
and all your old desire;
but in a queer tranquillity.
Yourselves. No reason any more
why not."

Part II

3 A.M. in New York

I have been standing at the edge
of this green field all night.
My hand is sticky with sugar.

The village winks; it thinks it is
the muscle of the world. The heart.
The mouth.

The horse is standing across the field, near the fence.
He doesn't come any closer,
even in the dark, or run away.

Blood memory:
fixed on vacancy:
coming back and back for a sign

the flat of his coat
the shut out of his eye.

Space

Keeping to my room
the cut in my thumb
took on more interest than the thumb

the dark a clean success
after the changing mask
of his face,

and my body—
its hypnotic
ticking over and over,

wanting, not wanting,
in all that hard-edged, squared-off, positive
concrete, aluminum.

I let it go,
all seven years and seven years.

I'm weightless, free   unwritten space

How do they get from minute to minute here?

Far off, low,
a little stir begins, a word, a missed

beat, a listening: this-
world, this-world.

Letter from a Country Room

Off without you
I hang around in the middle distance, walking, talking,
working   made-up mindwork
to send to the city Michael
where you are, where you write
    "She's coming back from the coast next week,
    I don't know what then"
A moth beats at the screen,
the thin, yellow dotted curtain lifts, tacked to the soft
scribbled-over wood   *signed QB + FB   8/15-(69)*
                       Nothing   Fuck War
                          To   No Peace, Jaybo?
                       Worry About

The sky streams hollowness, no city cover of light.
I follow, where they go,
someone's house,
I go, dim, incognito: tacked
to the way things are. Everything streams:
dumbstruck, stopped stock-still: you too: Jaybo!
Our quiet
trustful sides
pro
tec
ted
anyhow down the whole 200 miles.

A Child's Death

I remember the dark spaces,
black sand islands rising on the x-rays:
what I couldn't touch.

Not like this world,
our old solid,
where we multiply;

not this blurred body
merely her history.

Revolution

Here is a man.
Behind him
dark, in front of him
dark. The fuse the world lit

races up his spine. Blows up
his son who holds by him,
his love of women,
his learning   his wanting
late now to be touched   to touch.
An ordinary man. Thou
red black white slight scattered

thing o women's animal-song o slant
blown up drift arch dead white
song white powder   women rocking rocking
nowhere to lay your head
fox bird woman and man
o come   and out of nothing   whiteness
they come, tearing their shirts off,
alone, together, touching,
not touching, friends, who are the living
who were the dead?

Three Voices One Night in the Community Kitchen

A MAN:

"Jeb was hitting her in the face, I sat there, not doing anything.
Her face was open, as if he wasn't hurting her. He didn't look angry.
He sat back and they were smiling at each other. He knew her
better than I did. I wanted to kill Jeb, I didn't even get up. I haven't
even said what really happened."

A WOMAN:

"I was sitting in the back seat. Another woman we both knew, but
an old friend of his, was sitting in the front seat beside him. He was
shouting at her. She wanted me to help her, to get out, but then it
changed. She was alone in the car with him. He was driving.
She tried to touch his shoulder, he shrugged her off, he was looking
straight ahead, singing, talking to the drivers of the other cars."

A MAN:
"The books are all wrong. Besides you've never read them.
"You are another person.
"I've told you all about it, maybe you don't remember.
"I had a very long, very sad dream I just wanted to see a human face."

The Knife

In my sleep:
Fell at his feet   wanted to eat him right up
would have   but
even better
he talked to me.

Did I ask you to?
Were those words my blood-sucking too?

Now I will have a body again
move differently, easier   back to the plan
a little house   a woman and a man

crossed against yours my soul will show
glow through my breastbone:
Back down into the kitchen
yours

Here   I will save you
others have failed, even died, but I
will save you   you save me   devour me away
up

Woke up:
I can cry but I can't wake up
today again   don't answer the door
then did   couldn't look at you   talk

couldn't place the bed in the room, or where the room was
when I closed my eyes

This is the same old knife   my knife
I know it as well as I know my own mouth
It will be lying there on the desk if

I open my eyes I will know the room very well
there will be the little thrown-out globe of blood we left
and every molecule of every object here will swell
with life. And someone will be at the door.

Seeing L'Atalante

(Directed by Jean Vigo, 1934)

A woman sits at her worktable, reading stories,
thinking of all the true stories she'd never tell
out of love, and shame, root fear: broken glass, torn walls.
Reading stories about rivers (she is the river),
rafts crossing over, father, husband, lover,
her own sons. The river sings; he has always thought that. Stories.
The stories cross over.

On the raft he makes a shelter
for her, fills a glass (sees her trembling, clear),
tries to sleep.
Hours, hours, is he sleeping or swimming. Save her, save
them, leave them alone, his voice beats, his lungs, his heart,
his arms beat, beat, so slowly,   the wavering dark and the dark is
smiling, wanting their smile, their faces for its own.

Part III

Twenty Days' Journey by Huub Oosterhuis

Translated from the Dutch with Judith Herzberg

Twenty Days' Journey

I
I thought   it's only a thin threshold
a step scattered with straw.

It is a vertical stairway
a desert   steep with pyramids.

I edge down slopes. Dead bodies
shrug down past me. All their books.
Sentenced world, poisoned dream,
you are the most alone, the meanest.

The key I hold on to melts in my hand
I dig a pit
walk on   turn back
not a track anywhere

I bend to the wind
stalk this earth
hate my feet.

2
Wearing a veined marble vest
I sit at the game table, play,
play for life or death

for the blown-away footstep
in the snow
the voice that called me.

3
Who stumbles across the broken
field grass (foreground, left) and onto
the wide rusted wheel   falls   and then spins
and then stops   tries to think   runs on
across an island   am I.

The one who lies across the huge gold dome
(top center)   who lies   lips stretched to bursting
is you. Someone is still between us   almost
flesh   almost visible
tipped at the bottom of a blue-
brown river   like an old bottle.

4
Flood me then
stone that rushes red through the dam
fear tomorrow this moment
dry wood of imagining
dim awareness of *then*   now torn open
skinned alive.
My mind is lead, every cell
hard, heavy, metallic.

I climb up onto a road   trip
over the edge, fall

into your glass depth
you   beaker filled with fire

my body turns to mist but still stays alive,
an eye that will not close

5
20 days' journey: I pack vapor   fold air
make etchings of water on water
—see you standing there
but without a face   diamond death.

6
You are splintered into me
bits of soft denture
biting into my lips
useless pain   I am nothing   a brain pan
a cup holding your voice.
The chipped scales of your skin
crust my eyes closed
your palate slowly grows
into my mouth
your face grows out of my pores
like a feverish rash.
As if I never was
you cut your way out through every part of me
I become flesh of your flesh
bone of your bone.

7
Chalk lines still mark the floor
just where you stood. Our shoulders touched.
I was afraid. You were just saying
ordinary things.

Much became little   the mail
was left lying for days.
Nowhere now—
my sense of you everywhere

8
When they fired from the sea
onto a town
then   where the dead
stood on end like ropes
then   with the firing on Khe Sanh
it was then.

When a thin sac drifted down
out of the sky   hurled pillars
hands spattered   you called me

You had been living there a long time
you were taken
eyelids lips fingers and all
thrown against me
you   a bridge   a path through death.

I stood out in the sea, up to my waist in water
and took pictures of the fragments
the playing field   like a man's back.
The skipping survivors.

9
In small patches
it has clotted
become glass

something like a house
but empty

a shape
under a bright silk scarf.

I rub sand
into my eyes
so I won't see anything.

I hear you walk
as if you were carrying something:

your feet
grown back.

10
We walked
along the sea
the coastline broke like a thread.

I rang for days at the door
a long talk going on and on
through me like a wire

I crawled to the roof
where you were
when I got there you were gone.

Part IV

This Hate

It is like a fitting room only
with eight or nine
mirrors instead of three—

only, no door.
But you see: no ceiling. They never do.
I love them, my mother, my daughter. Both. I do, and I can write it
out and seal it

but it hurts, the mirrors closing in.
Now: the stamp.
I have to do this very carefully,
looking up; I feel, you see, the fontanel's   gentle
beat   at closing.

Carefully now—the shine is blinding—
I have to jump and drop it out, over.

Now I need a skin.
Or maybe this fogging up
transparency is it. Is it?
It feels like yours, more or less;
only for the face.

This Minute

The videotape runs
silent, but life-size.
A bed. A woman
and a man. A woman

and a man.
A woman and a woman.
An old man and a child.
A boy and a middle-aged woman.
Two women and a man
upside-down one
woman and two men

—The long black torn shades in the classroom
flicker like pigeons. The A/V man or his boy
shuts the windows.
—Coney Island   blurred
density   a still.

A bed again, a man
alone holding himself
there. Now a woman
sitting on the bed alone

writing on a filmstrip,
I'll ask when it's over
I think but
it starts over

with this time
—did they last time?—real
faces and breasts and
hands and crotches and

I stay to see it again
to see if it's me writing
it, that woman at the end,
that might make it easier or

not. Or I might be
one of the others.
Or not.—A siren goes by
down on the street, stiffening our spines.—No I'm not her

or anyone in it at all but here
it starts over and this time
—were they last time?—
all my friends.

You're in it this time,
and me, too,
but each off   alone   clear
in the shot that was a still,

Coney Island, but animated
now, walking
smoking
playing the transistor radio.

Watching, you
touch my hand
with the hand not holding the radio and say
you never loved me so much

as this minute. The A/V man
switches on the light, says "Quiet!" and I see
all our friends are here
watching. And here it starts over.

Couvre-Feu: *after Paul Eluard*

(in peacetime)

What could you expect
we were in a strange city, we saw no one,
we had almost no money, it was cold,
we went by different names, we hoped to see no one,
we went out mostly at night, it was cold,
what could you expect
on the streets they were all going home, carrying flowers,

every paper said you are doing these things
for the last time, every silence said
this has nowhere to go,

The green walls held.
We know what we knew
what could you expect
the narrow city
shone in all night on our room
what could you expect
we were one flesh one bone.

Fidelities

I
Up in this quiet room here, reading your letter,
it's as if I'm in your house. I'm reading.
You're working late, downstairs. The children are all asleep.
It's raining. Later we'll have some warm bourbon and water,
and sleep.
     Outside, the streets are white, the rain
shines like glass. Police
cruise by. You hold me in your arms.
Huge planes move off overhead.

It's as if
if I answer your letter I'll have to show them
my passport: New York. October.
Other friends, another life. It's as if I could choose.

2
strange, sad, these letters

not knowing what you're thinking, reading this

Friendships, fidelities.
Things as they are.
                                Out in the Sheep Meadow
I stare at the high school lovers lying, hardly moving, their skin
shining under the gray trees; I stare
at the old people, talking together, their faces
up to the sun. As if they were talking in bed.

My hand lying open in your hand . . .

The Sunday papers   the dreamy bicycle-riders

                                                As things are
I hate, I want to embrace the man, the woman who is near you,
who hears your step.

3
not even knowing where you are

Your quick, hunched-forward walk
in this man's walk, your eyes
in that old woman's gray, restless eyes.

4
We have our lives.

The river shone white-yellow under the yellow sky; every insect shone,
rising and dropping. We walked back up the field to the house.

Your room there. This white room. Books, papers, letters.
Stamps, the telephone. Our lives.
We're always choosing our lives.

5
All night I thought I heard the phone, or a child
crying. Your face
turned into a snapshot of your face, one
from five years ago.

Your wife and I were sitting up late
in the kitchen, drinking coffee, talking like sisters.
A child cried; one of us went to her, held her.

Here, sitting up late, with a friend,
listening, talking, touching her hand, his hand,
I touch your hand. No one
says anything much. No one leaves anyone.

Susan's Photograph

I am the razor that has been put away, also
the wrist in the photograph,
and—lately—also the photographer,
the friend, the taxi, the hospital room,
the three other women, their visitors, the flowers,
and the nurse.

At the end of that summer
I started going to paramedical school
at night. Days I still talk to my students
about all the dead
overexcitable poets; all their friends;
and the living; and show the old newsreels
where they keep leaving each other, old
people, children, soldiers; and the parades:
the general, the waving people, the black horses, the black
limousines, the mules, the tall gray puppets.

But this photograph here:
a woman in a country room, in western Massachusetts,
in peace, so sad and grained:
    now I see you look up, outside the frame—
this room here, friends, a table, a book or two,
paper, see you have all you need,

—even in prison you would have your childhood—
see you go on and do what you ought to do,

it is enough, now,
anywhere, with
everyone you love there to talk to.

Outside the Frame

It is enough, now, anywhere,
with everyone you love there to talk to.

And to listen.
Slowly we can tell each other some things about our lives:
runs, rests, brief resolutions; falls, and lulls;
hard joyful runs, in certainty; dull, sweet
durances, human silences;
                              look back in at the children,
the regular, neutral flicker of their blood; pale, solemn,
long-legged animal-gods in their sleep,
growing into their lives, in their sleep.

Forces (2): Song

Weeds breaking up through stone:
our hold on our own hollows, the quick,
curved line of a smile: bare, our own
ribs shelter us: a boy's cold, white
fingers around a match:
heart belling: hollow, quick,
through the live horn, the bone, to this
day, calm.

Notes

Page 103, "'*Autumn Day*'": "The house in the air . . ."

> Jung's autobiography, *Memories, Dreams, Reflections* (Vintage, recorded and edited by Aniela Jaffé); Chapter X, Visions. These ten pages record Jung's visions during three weeks after his heart attack in 1944. Particularly: "A short distance away I saw in space a tremendous dark block of stone, like a meteorite. It was about the size of my house, or even bigger. It was floating in space, and I myself was floating in space . . . I had the certainty that I was about to enter an illuminated room and would meet there all those people to whom I belong in reality" (pp. 290, 291).

Page 109, "Revolution": After Pontecorvo's film *Battle of Algiers*.

Page 123, "Susan's Photograph": "*—even in prison you would have your childhood—*"

> Rilke's *Letters to a Young Poet* (W. W. Norton): "And even if you were in some prison the walls of which let none of the sounds of the world come to your senses—would you not then still have your childhood . . . ?" (p. 18).

The Messenger

(1979)

My name comes to me like an angel.
—Tomas Tranströmer

Beka, 14

Squat, slant-eyed, speaking in phrase-book phrases, the messenger
says he is your brother, and settles down on his heels
to wait, muffled in flat, supple skin, rope over his shoulder. You
wait, play, turn, forget. Years,

years. The messenger is both like the penguin
who sits on the nest of pebbles, and the one
who brings home pebbles to the nest's edge in his beak,
one at a time, and also like the one
who is lying there, warm, who is going to break out soon:

becoming yourself: the messenger is growing
strong, tough feet for land,
and strong wings for the water, and long
butter-yellow feather eyebrows, for looks. And will speak,
calmly, words you already know: "thread," "island,"

"must": now, slowly, just while you lie on your cot there, half-
dozing, not reading, watching the trees,
a summer, and a summer; writing long pages, tearing them up;

lying there under the close August window, while at your back
the water-lit, dotted lines of home start coloring in.

Dufy Postcard

The postcard taped on your white kitchen wall has roses, in a white
bowl, on the blue and green shadowed table; the table is brown, yellow.
Down the wallpaper's field of pink roses, a violet shadow turns brown,
moves across the floor: now the lines go off the card, the lines of the
walls, one curved foot of the round table, the oblong shadow; the floor
ends mid-air, here:

You sitting at your table
looking at the postcard. Green
day lights the windows; everyone
still asleep. Taut lines.

Day, with its hours, and buildings;
people start, around you. You wait
a minute more in the white room—
white tent against the snowed-over path, the wind,
familiar voice—*one life*—

Every day you move farther outside
the outlines, kinder, more dangerous.
Where will you be going.
Who will the others be.

The Field

*"There is a strange power in bog water which prevents decay. Bodies have been found which
must have lain in bogs for more than a thousand years . . ."—A Danish Almanack of 1837.*
—P. V. Glob, *The Bog People*

A sculpture in a bare white gallery:
Pike jaws arch, in a shining transparent space
without locality: levels of peat, sand, air.
Bones. Teeth.
Fine, thin white jaws: the willingness to do harm—Odysseus
    leaving—

At forty we have always been parents; we hold each other's sex
in a new tenderness . . . As we were; hardly breathing
over the pulse in the infant's lucent temple—

Our breath comes shorter,
our lives have been a minute, a feather, our sex is chaff . . .

Sleep: the room
breaks up into blue and red
film, long muscles crossing bones, raw pelvis pulled
to birth: Incised on stone, bronze, silver
Eyes, belly, mouth   Circle on circle—

Look, by morning noises, in this city island flickering with gold flame,
These photographs.
The Tollund man. The Windeby girl. The goddess
Nerthus.

In the middle of a light wood   of tall forked trees stripped white
at the edge of a bog, in Denmark,
we walk   slowly out to the field   walk slowly by
the hacked-out cots
of silk
bog children.

Living Together

Dawn, streaks of rose-brown, dry—
A car starts up. A needle veers,
an hour, a summer . . . Day
settles back, on the last
century, our trying, our Biblical
conviviality.

This should, should not, happen, these
two people met, or not then, not now;
or now.

Out in the white Judaic light
you move like figures in a lesson;

You open your life like a book.
Still I hear your story

like a parable, where every word is simple,
but how does this one
go with the one before, the next . . .

Here Now

The sky is the same changing
colors as the farthest snow.
The tall pines float
like candles with the current,
next to the stream
clear with brown leaves.

    A pitched ceiling,
    two cots; apple petals;
    the thin smell of woodsmoke,
    wood, turpentine . . .
    My sister, I, who
    we were then—

    Downstairs, the grown world
    bent to its books; low flames, low
    voices. Sleeplessness . . .

    Our wooden room
    —The white cloth
    on the table between us

Forty years, a breath . . . our tall daughters circle like birds, in our
light houses, bump into things
Their high words, leaving out their lives

Quiet-minded, a lightness, this morning; the piece of sea glass next
to the window, almost amber, curved like a thumb, a petal

The sky is the same changing
blue, and green, as the burning snow.
So much must be asleep
under this white quiet, sleep,
sleep, low voices, dust hair,
under the eyes
the impossible
compass fingers
of the god.

The Forgiveness Dream: Man from the Warsaw Ghetto

He looked about six or seven, only much too thin.
It seemed right he would be there, but everything,
every lineation, was slow . . . He was speaking in Polish,
I couldn't answer him.
He pointed at the window, the trees, or the snow,
or our silver auditorium.

I said to him in English, "I've lived the whole time
here, in peace. A private life."   "In shame,"
I said. He nodded. He was old now, kind,
my age, or my mother's age: He nodded,
and wrote in my notebook—"Let it be good."

He frowned, and stopped,
as if he'd forgotten something,
and wrote again,
"Let it."

I walk, and stop, and walk—
touch the birch bark   shining, powdery, cold:
taste the snow, hot on my tongue—
pure cold, licked from the salt of my hand:

This quiet, these still unvisitable stars
move with choices.
Our kin are here.
Were here.

Turn

This is the new apartment   new
painted livingroom
its table, its bed, its chair.
It is floating, and the earth's bright rim
is floating through an indifferent blank, without
color, without consolation—

    The pregnant woman with a child at home
    rests, has a cup of tea, closes her eyes . . .
    I want to walk in the winter field again . . .
    Was peacefulness
    ever what we were after?
    She thinks of the child, who wants the tea, who wants
    her eyes, her mouth, her hands,
    who pulls her out to the field
    to the thick of things
    away from the thick of things.

A woman stands   at the new window.
Torso: a bronze Matisse back:
in the museum garden. Its children playing, still,
inside its hollow part.
Its strength thickens, simplifies.
Grows quieter.

The first day's quiet. The second; the second
year. I'm taking up my life. If you were here
who I am honest with

I'd have to think a long time
to say the simplest thing:
nothing like anything I know.

Prayer in Fever

The hospital shuts down to its half-night.

I stand back,
talk in words from some book:
The wall could be the floor.
Everything you look at
is changed by your looking at it

This packed dirt square, these wires . . . somewhere someone must
run for it, black hair, red mouth, burn
strips of fish on a green edge of the Hudson,
under a cloud of stars, under bridge lights, they must hunch down,
talk to each other, touch each other, the way this thin bright snow
masses, this blind oval pulling

gold   across the ceiling
floating out
off the fold-
back of space

The day does rise. The turning gaze of the river:
So many eyes. So calm.

The gray green curve of earth still
waiting   with us
holding us
huge curved mosaic hands

your hand
—how would you bide so long?

Working

in memory of Robert Lowell
1917–1977

Under the high rooms,
under the trains, the talk,
you kept digging down

from life to life
to come across earth's fragments:
the child; the century's children;

the ones we do not know yet,
because they were flesh —

their secret, lifted home-
voices, faces caught
in lightning.   Found there

earth's bone-shadowed eyes;
her still life
your awkward printing:

starvation: light
moving down and up through light . . .

A ladder of stuff: a soft, gray,
broken oar, a feather,
a shoe, a child's pencil case;

light drawing us
to light,
day speaking to day . . .

Now, at dusk
the man digging
saw himself approaching:

his half-smile looked past us: past himself:

the man chipping, at dusk,
under the trains, digging up
the dark, prosperous bluestone.

Silences: A Dream of Governments

From your eyes I thought
we could almost move   almost speak
But the way your face
held there, in the yellow air,
And that hand, writing down our names—
And the way the sun
shone right through us
Done with us

        Then
the plain astonishment—the air
broken open: just ourselves
sitting, talking; like always;
the kitchen window
propped open by the same
blue-gray dictionary.
August. Rain. A Tuesday.

Then, absence. The open room
suspended   The long street
gone off   quiet, dark.
The ocean floor. Slow
shapes glide by

Then, day
keeps beginning again: the same

stubborn pulse against the throat,
the same
listening for a human voice—
your name, my name

After Elegies (3)

Here in the close, most clear sun,
on this worn wood porch, halfway
over the beating harbor,
under the round sky—the daylight moon's
luminous, fragile skull—

Halfway between sleep and waking,
I think of you,
my old brother,
difficult friend; and your moving on
from us to the dead
seems a few blocks' walk;
seems nothing.

Are you nothing   Nowhere we can find you

—But you look up
from your spread-out books and papers, you say
—But now I can't hear what you're saying,
and how can you hear us now?
or see our rowing progress here? our bare arms
pulled—
          Earth pulled
to where it would not go.

The Messenger

I / THE FATHER
In the strange house
in the strange town
going barefoot past the parents' empty room
I hear the horses   the fire   the wheel   bone wings
your voice.

I make my corners:
this table
this letter
this walk.

The night you died
by the time I got there to the Peter Bent Brigham Hospital
the guard said, It's no use your going up.
That was the first time you spoke to me dead—
from the high corner of the lobby.

The next night a friend said, Well these deaths
bring our own deaths, close.

But now, this is your voice
younger than mine; leaning over—say goodbye—
the fake gold Navy officer's sword
the square real gun.

Every night the freight train crossed the grown-over road
at the foot of the Neilsens' field, trailing its rusty
whistle. The fire, the wheel; fireflies.
The wall of stars. Real horses. I could go
anywhere. I could go to where you are.

I lie under the bank, my face on the wall of wet grass.
I can't go anywhere, No such thing my dear.

My mother has flour on her hands,
on her cheekbone. My father smiles his one smile
gray and white on the wall. She pushes
her hair back from her eyes. His eyes
settle. On us.

II / THE MESSENGER
You are the messenger
my half-brother, I have seen you before,
you have visited me before,
in the hallways of a school, a hospital,
in a narrow hotel room once,
once on a dirt road in August.

I lean on the oak grain of this desk,
the grain of your body, your hair,
your long back. This plum
is darker than your mouth
I drink its salty sweetness   its leaf-smell
from your tongue. Sleep;
your dark head at my breasts

                                    turns
to a boy's head, you are Allan   my brother
Johnny DeSoto, nine
Philip   my brother
David

Your hand is my father's sure, square hand,
it is not too late, digging down through the sand
to show me the water

You turn, say something in your sleep

You are my sister   I hold you warm in my hand   her breast
You trace my breasts

My eyes were clenched, they are opening . . .
everything, nothing . . .
We aren't afraid.
The earth drips through us

Now I want to live forever
Now I could scatter my body easily
if it was any use

now that the earth
has rained through us
green   white
green green grass.

You say you came to say if I live without you
I'll live. That's always been your story.

III / THE HILL
The dogwood blossoms stand in still, horizontal planes
at the window. In mist. Small gray figures
climb away up the green hill. Carrying precision tools wrapped in
     oilcloth.
Some push their bicycles.—Wait, I'm coming, no this time I mean it

now I could scatter my body
if it was any use

saying again
if you do not teach me I shall not learn

—First, you see, you must be still. Touch nothing.
Here, in this room. To look at nothing, to listen to nothing.

A long time. First, you see, you must open your clenched hands.
You must carry your mother and your father at your breasts.

I stand on all fours, my fur
is warm; warm organs, the male and the female.
The earth is light and warm around us.
We lick our cracked old worries
like blood away from our faces, our haunches, we
nudge each other, all our white fur, goodbye, goodbye . . .

saying again there is a last
even of last times

I wake up with one hand holding hard to the other hand.
My head rests on oilcloth. A quiet voice laughs, and says again,

—You were going to go without me?
That was always your story.

Two Translations

Huub Oosterhuis:
Orpheus

Orpheus like a farmer
behind his plow of flutes
found in a dream the wound   the damp
place where the earth
quivers like a windpipe
and went down there.

Having been driven through woods
turned to rock   shifted by ice
fingers worn out with sailing
he got past the dog
and saw they were all dead there
except Eurydice.

Who lived in a barrel of zinc
brightly lit up
and had her love's doorframe
staves of a bed   a tree
swelling about her own underleaf white
sloping body
waiting for him but almost
unknowingly.

Enlisted with god he served seven years
shepherd   doorman   or he threaded wires
that would blow up thresholds   sink boats
direct the sun
and, to claim her, he became
wisely poorer.

Sometimes thought I'll walk into the countryside
like a horse

won't eat   will drown
it's better so
But did not want to and knew why not
the next day and the following he did his work
and waited.

After another seven years she could come along
it was as if he felt the worn spots
all over her
she had grown aimless
fat from sitting and sleeping
Could it be the snake   the thirst
he thought, when I play the flute
she may follow   she may
once again turn beautiful
as she used to be.

All right then she follows him
and why shouldn't she
she is nobody else and his tall back
is older is more hairy
but still the one she always
used to caress.

Then suddenly he no longer knew
whether it was she
the tune having escaped him
The forest as in every underworld
was doing well he saw
what had decayed was resurrected
He did not look back.

Sleeping they go on without a sound
She dreams   You and I were walking
I'm waking up
the skins over my eyes are still black
from waiting for your eyes   Look at me

if you love me she calls
Run still faster

Running on stripped nerves   I have
not looked around he calls and we shall
dearest see the earth
until our second death.
Over the water
sunlight blows before the wind
the grass is dark   creatures pass by
He walks and no longer knows
whether or not he did look back
and where the earth is
underneath   above

Osip Mandelstam:
394

Toward the empty earth
falling, one step faltering—
some sweetness, in this
unwilling hesitance—

she walks, keeping
just ahead of her friends,
the quick-footed girl,
the young man, one year younger.

A shy freedom draws her, her hobbled step
frees her, fires her, and it seems
the shining riddle in her walk
wants to hold her back:

the riddle, that this spring weather
is for us the first mother:

the mother of the grave.
And this will keep on beginning forever.

There are women,
the damp earth's flesh and blood:
every step they take, a cry,
a deep steel drum.

It is their calling
to accompany those who have died;
and to be there, the first
to greet the resurrected.

To ask for their tenderness
would be a trespass against them;
but to go off, away from them—
no one has the strength.

Today an angel; tomorrow
worms, and the grave;
and the days after
only lines in chalk.

The step you took
no longer there to take.

Flowers are deathless. Heaven is round.
And everything to be is only a promise.
                              —Voronezh. 4 May 1937

Solitudes

*Some of the signs suggest that you feel a leaf or
other part of a plant. A string leads from the top
of the sign to the plant.*
　　　　　—Braille sign on the
　　　　　　Miwok Trail, Muir Woods

The bird a nest, the spider a web, man friendship.
　　　　　　　　　　—Blake

December 21st

How will I think of you
"God-with-us"
a name: a word

and trees paths stars this earth
how will I think of them

and the dead I love　　and all absent friends
here-with-me

and table: hand: white coffee mug:
a northern still life:

and you
without a body

quietness

and the infant's red-brown mouth　　a star
at the star of a girl's nipple . . .

Sanctuary

People pray to each other. The way I say "you" to someone else,
respectfully, intimately, desperately. The way someone says
"you" to me, hopefully, expectantly, intensely . . .
—Huub Oosterhuis

You   who I don't know   I don't know how to talk to you

—What is it like for you there?

Here . . . well, wanting solitude; and talk; friendship—
The uses of solitude. To imagine; to hear.
Learning braille. To imagine other solitudes.
But they will not be mine;
to wait, in the quiet; not to scatter the voices—

What are you afraid of?

What will happen. All this leaving. And meetings, yes. But death.
What happens when you die?

". . . not scatter the voices,"

Drown out. Not make a house, out of my own words. To be quiet in
another throat; other eyes; listen for what it is like there. What
word. What silence. Allowing. Uncertain: to drift, in the
restlessness . . . Repose. To run like water—

What is it like there, right now?

Listen: the crowding of the street; the room. Everyone hunches in
against the crowding; holding their breath: against dread.

What do you dread?

What happens when you die?

What do you dread, in this room, now?

Not listening. Now. Not watching. Safe inside my own skin.
To die, not having listened. Not having asked . . . To have scattered
life.

Yes I know: the thread you have to keep finding, over again, to
follow it back to life; I know. Impossible, sometimes.

What Happened

I don't know what happened, some very low time for my friend;
she said, — Come over; she couldn't talk, but come over anyhow.

My friend, have I ever befriended you? Helper and friend, will you
be befriended?

You talked along, quickly, forceably, about this thing and that, as
you do; you handed me coffee; I felt as if we were traveling at
some speed; in a taxi; I was looking at you through glass, you
looked back at me now and then, for a minute, through the glass;
so much grief in your eyes. Almost disinterested—

I asked, — What happened? Then, in your rush of talk, you told
me stories, about old friends, people you met, you showed me books,
photographs I'd like, you fed me, you entertained me.

Am I the unknowable one? Does my listening make just a white
place, like the space a person who is growing blind sees growing on
the page?

Suddenly you stopped walking around the room, stopped smiling.
You sat down, across from me; you said,
    — You and I are the same, in terrible ways.

Then furiously, talking very fast, you told me about my life:
How I go on repeating, over and over, my stupid leap for
home, where there's nothing; a homeless world; what else
did I think I was doing with X, last year; what good did
I think work could do; or anything else; knowing now how
things are: what would I do?

Telling me about your life:
It's always like that: you leap, you think for a minute you
have found something; Nothing; Terrible; there are only
distractions, crowding around over the surface of things.
—Now what would I do. People don't kill themselves, just
because they know how things are, know the world is
like this; they aren't so rational.
Asking yourself:
—What would you do—

To wait. To imagine . . . I just sat there, blind; not-there;
my friend, and I, not seeing each other; seeing instead some mask
or sign; consenting to be some mask or sign.
The half-cured man in Mark's gospel, who answers Christ, "I can
see men as if they were trees, but walking."
To not see, not be seen: the sudden fear: like a déjà vu: is there
anyone I do see? anyone I know? even of the closest ones. Or who
knows me?

To listen for what it is like there. To wait . . . Contagion: our grief
and fury ran down like electricity into the ground, leaving the
room a fiction, an empty space. The glass didn't shift, we
couldn't touch only ghosts: the unreachable teller, the unreachable
listener; both going silent, unbefriended.

—But there are shelters; they break down, but they mend; we
can live, that way. But I didn't say anything; you were telling me
another story, smiling your strong smile, showing me more
things: I couldn't get past them; there wasn't time.

I keep talking to you, here, in my head; but I don't know what to
say: not enough:

Yet the cell is only the rudiment. A human being is made up of
about 1,000 billion cells, a drop of blood containing 5 million
of them . . .

To wait. To imagine. Learning braille.

Once I was talking to a friend, a religious man, about the closeness
of friendships in childhood, and he said, What you're talking
about, is God. Mercy on our gropings, our silences. Our harm.
Mercy, or nothing is enough; mercy on our deceptions, endless, our
endless longings; our words that go like smoke into smoke. Some
shelter,
for my friend,
for each one, quiet, talking,
alone, together, to trust, to rest in a while.

Turn (2): After Years

January. At the window
wet-dark twigs and branches of young birch
reach up, cross each other:
a road map, a map of rivers . . .

Hundreds of drops of the freezing rain
hold the day's gray light close:
silver   hundreds of stars

I think of you
looking out your city window—everyone away
—a thin, light-eyed, noticing child,
standing so quiet

—a tall man, restless, faithful, your light eyes always
not-here; always here . . .

I think of our lives
different   the same

the years, half-blown,
   What we had, we have.

Now I can turn,
—now, without want, or harm—
turn back to the room, say your name:
say: *other*   say, *thou* . . .

The Burden of Memory

Do you remember, last time we saw each other, how the first thing
you said was, "Isn't it good we're always friends?" And then, both
of us, I think, feeling stopped, empty-handed; past the high,
brittle day of meeting like lovers, five years ago; just ourselves
again, groping for friendship again. And then, you talked so
easily, like when we were kids; more than you ever have, to me,
about your life, now; yourself.

And I remembered, what I'd known before—I wonder if it's so, for
you, too—being drawn, with you, by memory, back to a life that
seems less harmful . . . "student days" . . .—And what good was
that? That memory itself drawing us to harm.   But then,
ourselves again; some mercy; taking in that angry sorrow, part of
us, a healed bone that does go on hurting; a mark of mercy; and
we could be quiet again, and talk.

And then, here in this solitude, this quiet, remembering so many
things I'd forgotten, I was thinking back to those days: you, an
"older man," going with L.; I suppose you were both seventeen . . .
Do you remember, one day when we were talking, I forget what

about, but my saying, "You're such a friend to me," and you said,
"Yes and I always will be." And then I could tell you about that
time, in California.—I want to talk to you now about it, again;
I've never talked to anyone else about it, and it's been alive with
me here again—do you remember it? I don't think you could;
the whole family, over at another Navy family's place, for a picnic.
1943—I was nine. I was off from the other kids when I saw it. In
a shed, or garage, I don't remember: a wooden building, pretty far
off from the house. There was a barrel, but I could see into it, and
there were heads in there, people's heads, cut in half. In something
like formaldehyde maybe, they were kept so life-like. I never knew
why I didn't run for one of the other kids, to look.—I could only
finally tell, on the way home; I got sick again, in the car, and I
told them. Of course my parents said Nonsense, it was impossible;
but very angry. A little later they said I must be very overtired,
and after that they were always very careful that I should get
plenty of sleep.—I could never tell anyone again. It was so real:
but it *was* impossible, it couldn't have been there. I must be
crazy. And what a creepy kind of crazy. What becomes of people
like that?—And some awful shame, worse than any shame I've
ever felt.

And then I could tell you, that day, ask you, if you thought I was
crazy; tell you about the shame. And you said, "I think it happened.
In some way. I don't know. It doesn't matter, what way."

—You mean a dream or something. I *know* it wasn't a dream. But
I know, it couldn't—

—We were around the same age. I saw things . . . we heard about
things.

—But you were there, in the war.

—It doesn't matter. I don't know. It was 1943. People knew things.
We do; we know things now. And here we are, alive. Fine; playing,
in peace. No wonder for the shame. What will we do? I don't
know . . . But it doesn't mean we did those things. *You* know that.

I wonder if you had any idea, how saving that was, what you said.

The same lightening of things, talking to you now, in this room—

And you—I wonder, have I been companionable to you, too,
been there, any use, in your silences, your aloneness—your letter
the other day, saying, "a low time"—I wish I could touch your
hand, there, now . . .

—*We do know things.* That memory, back with me now, and the
shame. Now. *What will we do*

How long can we stay interested in the lone man's liberty? . . .
I'm afraid [the individual], being saved by himself, will be lost
by himself . . .—Montale

February 9th

The consolation of another solitude, miles away, years away; in
the next room; its words, its silences;
waiting to be listened for; imagined.
Kinship.   Meetings.

We all line up to ask each other for help.
Millions.
One.
        Line up—in Swedish—associations of people lining up for food,
        shelter . . .—Tranströmer
My whole life, I've never been hungry. Or without a room; with
warmth, and light. Warm; fed. At the edges of this world. People
who *are driven out of their minds by good living.*—Milosz

Aloneness: physical feelings: cold, hunger.   Wrongfulness.
Solitude—choosing to hope to live—holding close in the cold

Emily Dickinson: *. . . test's severe repairs are permitted all.*
                    . . . It is difficult not to be fictitious in so fair a
                    place, but test's severe repairs are permitted all.

Not to be fictitious.
I can't think of the first word.

Uncovering; unthickening. Changes
. . . the memories I can't look out past, to look around: this room—

Look: they join you to every fragility   here

Your letter, from August: *At the same time*
there is such a strong sense, of uncovering
and naming to the point of losing what you
may have had . . . It was like touching the
center and therefore losing it, emptying it
of what you might have been able to hold on to.

    And your letter, saying, *No one has*
    ever asked me about "everyday life" . . .
    Raising your son, teaching, in Maine,
    alone painting, paintings not seen
    changing   your memories changing
    We must account for our existence
    and it helps to talk openly if at all
    possible. I will try,

And your letter, saying, *We are*
indeed graced by our mutual friendship
with B_____. She has saved my life more
than once and most especially this fall.
No doubt you have heard from her about

    And you, writing, this letter today,
    the hidden way of each of us, buried

    kinship
    a buried crystal holding the sun

    kinship
    the salt of our hands
    touching

changing

memories changing

Higginson: *. . . I have the greatest desire to see you, always feeling*
that perhaps if I could once take you by the hand I
might be something to you;

Dickinson: *You were not aware that you saved my Life.*

"Love and Work":
Freud Dying

—London, September 1939

He could watch his soul, a line drawing, almost a cartoon, rise up,
out of his mouth, past the footpaths up a steep, concentric
mountain, to enter another city: a vast, black and white city,
at the top of space, precisely edged in blue and red and gold leaf.
September. A gray, light absence of God.

All his books were there, in his room; and the rugs over the sofas,
and the small Egyptian statues, the Greek heads. Men and women
with sad, lively eyes came and asked to study with him. Friends
and colleagues were there, "both of the past & of the present."

But the first hour, resting for a minute, from his walk, on a bench
in a green square near his house, he fell asleep. He dreamed he
was walking, deep in the ocean; he was both male and female.
The dome of the world fitted perfectly over the ocean floor. The
slow currents filled his mind with a reasoning peacefulness he
thought he must remember. High clouds of sunlight moved through
the water.

No one here was marked off, by coloring or sex or money. Still, as
they walked slowly by him, their faces held some questioning,
calm sorrow. The dream was like a voice, the singsong rhythms of

a voice he had known a long time, but without words, an old
story. He wondered if someone had told it to him.

He woke up: he wanted to touch someone; to listen, again, to the
consolation of that voice. Familiar voices waited around him in
his room. One spoke his name, a strange sounding word, now.
Most he wanted, to go back to his dream, where there were no Jews,
no saving needed,
and no fame of accomplishment to save them.

No, it must just be that he didn't know anything yet, about that
strange, slow place, its darknesses; he had to go back and listen;
walk there, and think:

Letter from a Stranger

You said, you know what I mean: one winter, you looked and saw
a river branching in the black sycamore branches, silver
veins of roads rising and ending in icy twigs at your window;
an awful time. Then spring came and you said
you learned to love Lincoln again; the first leaves came
and you saw Lincoln's *kind, grave face, drawn there*
in the leaves, in the light.
How can I answer your letter? words from your life
bring me home to my life. So safe
now, that I can leave it again, now
the milky quiet. The warm straw.

"Actuarial File"

Orange peels, burned letters, the car lights shining on the grass,
everything goes somewhere—and everything we do—nothing

ever disappears. But changes. The roar of the sun in photographs. Inching shorelines. Ice lines. The cells of our skin; our meetings, our solitudes. Our eyes.

A bee careens at the window here; flies out, released: a life without harm, without shame.   That woman, my friend, circling against her life, a married life; that man, my friend, solitary, anarchic, driving away from home; them driving, to each other—

I know, the hard, half-lost, knowing will; the cold first loneliness again, outside the commonweal, unmoving;

But to say, *I know*—is there any touch in it?

> The words in my dream: "actuarial file." *Actuary, 1. A registrar or notary, who keeps records of the acts of a court . . .*

To be there; to listen; not invade. Another solitude . . .

I watch her face. The lines of will, kindness, hunger. Silence. She moves from one thing to another thing in the kitchen, looks out the window at the other apartment windows . . . A woman moves around, across the courtyard, making supper. How many people is she making supper for? Now the woman waters the plants. What is she thinking about. Her head, her arm, look peaceful . . .

"*Everything that happens, happens once and for all.* Is this true? If so, what then?"

Yes. Your story; all of your hope; what you do, breaks. Changes. "If so, what then?" Nothing disappears. And you do last;

The words in the open page of her notebook, *I'm so cold. My head hurts.*

Come stay here, at my place, a while.—Someday we will be able to say, I did this thing; I did that other thing; I was that woman.

Someday, we will be able to take it in, that violence, hold it in our
hands . . . And the ones who come after us, maybe they can
understand us; forgive us; as we do forgive our parents, our
grandparents, moving so distantly through their lives . . . their
silences . . .
And the ones we were with   maybe our friendship can change,
can mend . . .

Come stay here. Things change . . .

She stays home;

Not to invade   Wait, here, in the quiet

Lines from a Story

*I remembered . . . [my grandfather] said that if you let your blood
run, you make yourself better. If there are spirits in you that
want to go, they will leave with the blood.*
—An Eskimo woman, to Robert Coles

Mother   your quiet face
already at eight years old a survivor's face:

You say   there is no mother or father,
say, fear,   It is too cold
here, you say, I am alive,   I will
hold myself in my own hands.

The white beach in that photograph, white
lake, white sky, a page . . .   your story
that I know in such spent outlines . . .

But still your hands
hold me to you, here,

your voice reads to me, still,
—your voice that forgot itself
in other people's words—

You never thought you knew things.

And I have begun, so late, to trust what I love!
To hope
to gather in the rest.
Or let it go:
I cut my arm, it bled;
a long dawn
opening to here:

in my own hands
in the quiet   listening
—I send this page to you,
from memory:
lines from a story, about two friends
who lived in distant towns:
"—If I could talk to you now,
I believe we could be so simple,
if you could talk to me,
then we could be so still."

March 21st

Out of 92 natural elements, we could never have predicted man. We could never even get to the wetness of water, the miracle of ordinary water. Water is one of the strangest substances in all of chemistry.
—George Wald

5 A.M.

Waking. Something, dry, without shape, moving toward the tilted faces, the voices, of the dream,

The room the clearing in the trees moving

Now, the thumbed line of daylight, behind them,
finding the room,   its lines, down, across—
my body   finding again   "I"

The words from a dream of yours, twenty years ago,
"Relay locality"

And you, my father, my brother, your face in my dream, receding,
your voice saying, what they told me you did say,
— *They're getting farther away; but it isn't them, it's me; I'm
getting old;*

Your voice, leaving: and still the day

And you, my brother,
— *No wonder for the shame.*

And you, my mother, my sister,
our talk   our stillness   now

And you, my father, my mother,
"unlosable friend"

saying again
— *Here is the life outside the window,
   here is the earth, the water, here is
   fire, the blood, the breath moving through your own hands*:

   your work   everyone you love

And you, my sister, writing,
the hidden way of each of us, buried

To drift   allowing

forgetting my name   my life

the salt of our hands
touching

changing:

over and over: following

you   who I don't know
listening: changing

the play of the breath of the world

they   he   she   you

Notes

THE MESSENGER
Pages 141 and 142: "saying again
                    if you do not teach me I shall not learn"

        and

        "saying again there is a last
        even of last times"
                —Samuel Beckett, "Cascando,"
                from *Poems in English*

Page 145: The poem by Osip Mandelstam was translated with Anne Frydman.

Home.Deep.Blue

(1989)

Willi, Home

In memory

Last night, just before sleep, this: a bright
daffodil
lying in bed, with the sheet pulled up to its chin.
Willi, did I ever know you? The shine
in the lamplight!   of your intelligent glasses,
round and humorous.
Did I ever know myself? When I
start bullshitting I see your eyebrows fly . . . This book
is dedicated to Willi,
whom I do not know,

whom I know. The words in my head
this morning
(these words came from an angel):
"It's too late to say goodbye.
And there are never enough goodbyes."
I know: the daffodil
is me. Brave. Willi's an iris. Brave.
Brave. Tall. Home. Deep. Blue.

To Raphael, angel of happy meeting

The pear tree buds shine like salt;
the stretch of new-ploughed earth holds up
five colors of brown to the strict sun —
like an old woman's open hand, at rest.

The young people of this house wake up,
one by one, they set out . . .

Further away, still their voices hold,
across the fog; and the pull of the ropes
— these branches rubbing in the rain —

Further away, the full sails   grains of salt
thrown into the wind . . .

The pear tree prints its buds
across my back, my hands,
bright drops of light, in the wind. Light,

Break through this husk, this
mask of 'Goodbye' . . .

Why was I crying?   It was as if
some courteous hand
had touched my eyes, and I saw,

in that thin Sixties backyard
in Seattle, the abundant tree
open out its branches, white-gold wings
protective of our waiting,
of our wishes, still too light for us to hold.

Primitive Painting: Liberation Day

Everyone is wearing work clothes, old clothes, boots; and old uni-
forms, painted green and brown, like trees. The new government has
asked everyone to assemble in the center of the Old City, and has
given everyone small ribbons to wear, stiff flowers.

Two men in business suits are pouring wine into cups, at a long trestle
table; a few of the men and women have begun to drink.

At the bottom corner of the painting is a row of bright green leaves,
like a signature. A tall man, in the foreground, looks straight out into
the painter's eyes; his hands are crossed over his genitals. There are no
children, or animals, in this picture; no one makes a sound, or has
another side.

This is a desert, and they call it peace, this is Liberation Day; the new government is drunk again, and the painter's fear is white in his paint.

Awake, This Summer

I see you a minute, a year ago, at the door
of our friend's empty room,
your eyes, the slanted-back weight of your body,

moseying around. That night, your hand
jumped in your sleep, you said
"Everyone was friends" . . .

Late summer mornings
I slept in your side, in the sun,
and to all your wishes in my sleep I wished "Yes."

A year's ocean of sleep we moved in,
without air; no one
was friends.

        Awake, this summer, first
finished with that, my chest hurts, and
the shallowest breath is life.

Mandelstam

*1934–35. The time of his arrest and imprisonment in Moscow,
and his exile, with his wife Nadezhda Jakolevna Khazina, to
Voronezh.*

My mother's house
Russia

Calm are the wolf's bronze udders,
calm the light around her
fur, out-starred with frost

I am 43
Moscow we will not live

Russia
Iron shoe
its little
incurved length and width

Russia   old
root cellar   old mouth of
blood under-the-earth
pulling us down into herself
no room to lie down

    and your poor hand
    over and over
    draws my brain
    back to your breast's small
    campfire

Voronezh we won't live
    not even my hand
    to hold to your hand, useless.

The Drinker's Wife Writes Back

You never hear me, your letter said.
But I was the one who always listened
and understood, reliable, listening
at your thought's door . . . I was steady
as the oak our bed is made of . . .

The name of a good doctor, your letter said.
I wait in his green waiting room;
my hands are big, pale, idle. Neutral, intent,
his secretary calls me 'Dear,'
like one of my own children.

He is kind. I can't last out the hour.
The window panes behind him stare me down,
the lenses over his eyes. He asks, What brings me here?
But I feel—not naked—
but absent, made of air

because how could I ever have told
anyone how it was, how the lighted house
went out in the gin brightness
you called 'the war'—and that I did this to you—
I did not do this . . .

Birthday Letter from South Carolina

for Sarah, 21

Yellow apple
star inside the apple
seed star   quiet

Walking up this quiet, red-earth road,
I think of you there, near the white-
edged harbor; in a yellow kerchief,
in the blowing sunlight, you walk
along the concrete of the holding world.

You hold it all to your chest, the blue day, night,
long reading, long talk,   —You hold
your kind, stumbling, sure

life in your hands.
Indian cloth, the goose-neck desk light . . .

Basho spent the first thirty years of his life
apprenticing; four years alone in a small hut
on the outskirts of Tokyo;
the last ten years
walking. Walking here

today I saw him, Basho, at the far edge of the field;
and you alongside him; your steps,
his long black and white steps stirring up
red mica dust to drift across the new day's light, and the heat.

The Counselor Retires, and Then He Dies

Getting each other's jokes,
each other's absences; my first wise
practice at intimacy; and now the hero
shrugs on his London raincoat and walks away,
down the shiny street: it's a death, Doc.

No more of
you in your pale green office, your bright green pants,
your lounging, affectionate smile, you
cradling your dog when he had a cold,
the way you would cradle me, if I was a dog,
or a baby, the way God cradles us,
only we can't feel it . . .

Shea,
guard me and keep me,
as I keep you;

let me go, and I
let you go: a white balloon magic-markered *Shea*
floating up the white sky.

Juliana

Our lives went differently,
we lost touch . . .

The table is solid,
its long cloth shines.
Husband and wife lived in one house, forever,
and this was nothing wonderful, a simple fact.
Grown children gather, they bring
white tulips, forsythia.

All the guests make toasts. Sex taps at our sleeping ears
like water in another room . . .

The couples lean back, rich canvases. My hunger plays
in front of them, empty,—dozes off, day-dreaming
of true desire.
I try waking, try saying,

Well, we're all human,
                              —One outlying face smiles
and leans forward, gray and mild . . .

Later Juliana
I meet you, a minute, on the stairs,
and you stop, and hold my arms,
and tears run down your face . . .

Just waking up
she didn't remember what time of year it was,
and couldn't remember if she had a friend
in the world, Oh thank God, summer, and she remembered last night
her husband's friend, the professor,
that he said, Waiting is what we do, in this life, we wait.

Visit

This warm house, masculine; our old,
20-years-old hug;
your gray eyes, that I trust.
But our clear,
perfect sentences,
like money. No silences.

Jokes, books, our friends . . .
Why are you always
the older one? Why am I
a wooden girl, not
friends when we meet?

   The other one, tough, dumb,
   kind, the monologuer,
   the strange one, with no house
   —after our first fight
   we didn't have to have that fight anymore,
   or go away.

Solid perfect waves
break in and pull back.

It was as if you shouted after me,
"Can't you see my death, can't you see anything?"

Snow Landscape, in a Glass Globe

In memory of Elizabeth Bishop

A thumb's-length landscape: Snow, on a hill
in China. I turn the glass ball over in my hand,
and watch the snow
blow around the Chinese woman,
calm at her work,
carrying her heavy yoke
uphill, towards the distant house.
Looking out through the thick glass ball
she would see the lines of my hand,
unearthly winter trees, unmoving, behind the snow . . .

No more elders.
The Boston snow grays and softens
the streets where you were . . .
Trees older than you, alive.

The snow is over and the sky is light.
Pale, pale blue distance . . .
Is there an east? A west? A river?
There, can we live right?

I look back in through the glass. You,
in China, I can talk to you.
The snow has settled; but it's cold
there, where you are.

What are you carrying?
For the sake of what? through such hard wind
and light.
          —And you look out to me,
and you say, "Only the same as everyone; your breath,
your words, move with mine,
under and over this glass; we who were born
and lived on the living earth."

Everything Starts with a Letter

Everything starts with a letter,
even in dreams and in the movies . . . Take
J. Juliana, on a summer afternoon,
in a white silk blouse, and a pale blue-flowered skirt,
—her shoes? blue? but high and narrow heels,
because she asks Sam to carry the plate of Triscuits
into the garden, because she can't manage
the brick path in her heels.
"Oh could you? I can't manage the path in these heels."

J is the letter my name begins with,
O is the letter for the moon,
and my rage shines in my throat like the moon!
Her phoniness, O my double, your and
my phoniness . . .
Now what shall we do?
For this is how women begin to shoot,
we begin with our own feet, men empty their hearts, oh
the false self will do much worse than that,
to get away . . .

About Love

1
No   when you went to her
(oh when she told me so) then I turned to
her   her   her   her: emptiness:

black hollows falling over alone
under the white running water

2
"Light as milk in a child's cup,
I will hold you, at my lips

I will feed you," said the soft black pelican
about love, the mother, God the pelican,
the mother, stem of all our tenderness.

3
Ribbon of the
silver path of the milky
light on the water, how
you follow yourself across my mouth,
across my hair;

beads of water,
bright tall necklace of light, how you
thread yourself through me, through
my lips, their silk
stem.

Little Song in Indian Summer

I am
is my name and your name, *I am* is
the name we are finding,
I am is the
name who is finding us, is
(standing still in the high grass, in the hot sun)
the one I always wanted to find, is
the one I always wanted to find,
not mother, not child, oh you
I need
who are glad
I am I
with your green eyes even
with welcome, with letting go.

The King

You take the card of your self out
at the green crossroads, you
pull your name close around you.
But whose words are you speaking? Whose
money is this? Your warm
mouth on my mouth stuns me, your hand
on my breast is so bright, I
have to shut my eyes . . .

Still I won't take the card you offer,
though its coin is highly prized,
and its coin is wild,
—its coin is "Mine be mine,"
its coin is "And I will love you then,"
its coin was death
to the thirsty child
not heard but drowned in the deep sea . . .

High School Boyfriend

You were willing to like me, and I did something,
and blew it,
and your liking me would have saved me,
and my liking you would have saved you,

that was the circle I was walking around,
pushing a bar that moved a wheel
down in the dark, holding my breath,
naked in a long hard army coat of you,
hating my feet, hating my path . . .

Today my tongue is a fish's tongue,
kissing my friend's light breastbone, his chestnut down;
full of tears, full of light, half both,
nowhere near my old home: no one anywhere
is so wrong.

Tonight I Can Write. . .

after Pablo Neruda

Tonight I can write the lightest lines.

Write, for example, 'The evening is warm
and the white mist holds our houses close.'

The little evening wind walks in the field grass
and hums into her own chest.

Tonight I can write the lightest lines.
I love him, and I think he loves me too.

He first came to me on an evening like this one
and held me in his arms.

He kissed me again and again then,
under the motherly bending down stars.

He loves me, and I think I love him too.
How could one not love his calm eyes, as blue as the earth.

Tonight I can write the lightest lines.
To think that I did not know him, that now I am beginning to know him.

To feel the warm lamplight: soon it will warm his brown arm.
'And the verse falls to the soul like dew to the pasture . . . '

Trust Me

Who did I write last night? leaning
over this yellow pad, here, inside,
making blue chicken tracks: two
sets of blue footprints, tracking out
on a yellow ground,
child's colors.

Who am I?
who want so much to move
like a fish through water,
through life . . .
                Fish *like* to be
underwater.

Fish move through fish! Who
are you?

And Trust Me said, There's another way to go,
we'll go by the river which is frozen under the snow;

my shining, your shining life draws close, draws closer,
God fills us as a woman fills a pitcher.

The River at Wolf

(1992)

X

I have decorated this banner to honor my brother. Our parents did not want his name used publicly.
—from an unnamed child's banner in the AIDS Memorial Quilt.

The boatpond, broken off, looks back at the sky.
I remember looking at you, X, this way,
taking in your red hair, your eyes' light, and I miss you
so. I know,
you are you, and real, standing there in the doorway,
whether dead or whether living, real.—Then Y
said, "Who will remember me three years after I die?
What is there for my eye
to read then?"
The lamb should not have given
his wool.
He was so small. At the end, X, you were so small.
Playing with a stone
on your bedspread at the edge of the ocean.

Spring and Its Flowers

Then, *Tell me your fantasies,* you said.
And I: *OK; I'm lying in bed, asleep, a child,*
and you, you're sitting in the rocker there, knitting,
like a mother bear. And you:
Can I be the one in the bed, too?
And you in the chair there, knitting?

That February you dreamed your old father said, *Spring*
this year and its flowers
will cost you eighteen thousand dollars.
Waking up we wished we could have lived together
in a green and blue walled garden forever . . .

We didn't know
we were so close
to the world's mouth, the drunk bear's ashy thing.

The Summer Was Not Long Enough

Stanley, my ex, the painter,
stepped out of his van.
His beard was gone. Loudly, carefully,
he started to paint the trees
and the ground and the telephone poles
grass green.

Funny, I was crying
after him: not Stan's upsidedown-ness,
my own. My own friends, not written back,
not called. Oh our love
turned from, and August half over.

August's more than half over;
Dove, it's time for peace.
Time to taste the round mountains, the white and green,
and the dusk rose of relationship, again,
for the first time, it's time to take off our clothes,
and the fortresses around our eyes, to touch our first fingers,
you and I, like God, across everything.

Still Life, for Matisse

Light
old leaf spine
fish spine bone
green under-the-

ocean light
big gold fish my
new little father
only a boy
breathing on the window
COME ON OUT
you carry me I carry you
light wave after wave
swim cockatoo
green, blue.

Still Life: in the Epidemic

Light
old leaf spine
fish spine bone
green under-the-
ocean light

big gold fish my
new little father
only a boy
breathing on the window
COME ON OUT,

My eggful of eggs
floating opening
up in your cream, up in
your blood,
Are you sick? Are you well?

A blood sample will be taken from your
arm with a needle and analyzed in a
laboratory using a test called ELISA
(enzyme-linked immunosorbent assay).

If the ELISA test is positive, a
second test, called Western Blot, will
be run on the same blood sample to
confirm the result.

The palm of your glove is
powder on my mouth, powder in my fear,
your rough tongue your talk
is warm on the cool hospital issue
black silk blindfold crackhouse blindfold

you green in the dark tying a rubber
strap around my arm playing the radio
your heavy head, green in the dark.
Are you still in the room?
Are you still in the house?

Then you, Doctor,
you say sincerely,
"You can always go on suicide neutral,
then everyone, from both sides, from his side and her side,
will leave you alone." And Mother

State, you say, "You are not enough.
I am. Eat me, and
I will raise you up. On TV, eat me.
Chew me, gingerly, like chewing ice,
eat me. America. Eat me."

Ikon

Swim in you, sleep
in you, let me,
Mother Lord,
all this hour

—I am your cloth of gold
swaddled firstchild
safe in danger
(you are in danger)

one hand curled around your
bending neck, the other
rested on your black breast,
just above your star.

Winter in the world
is winter here in you
but summer, too,

oh my play,
my eyes, my light. Black
hill of consolation! There is no book
and my name is written in it, my heart makes
an earth crib for your heart.

The Year of the Snake

I had to ask you questions: if I didn't, well
you'd think I'd robbed a bank. And then, blood all over, God,
I would've robbed a bank. But my old God,
my questions were too small for you. You
were so much older, you *knew* so much. You
used your words like bricks, whole leathery old
books black with words, to wall me out, words gold
as booze, to leave the room, leave me, leave us. Oh
since that time, I have learned
to let you go and live . . .

Now my friend happy as God I sit down and comb your hair.
Your hair shines like honey like sex like the current in the river.

The river combs out our anger our tenderness.
Our silent tenderness not *my* or *mine* or *yours*.
Your unspeaking mouth shining.
Shining lifesnake drinking at my lips milky with life.

The One You Wanted to Be Is the One You Are

She saying, You don't have to do anything,
you don't even have to be, you Only who are,
you nobody from nowhere,
without one sin or one good quality,
without one book, without one word,
without even a comb, you!
The one you wanted to be
is the one you are. Come play . . .

And he saying,
Look at me!
I don't know how . . .

Their breath like a tree's breath. Their silence
like a deer's silence. Tolstoy
wrote about this: all misunderstanding.

Ironwood

November 17th
Dear Michael,
    I had gotten *Ironwood, The Final Issue,* in the mail; I put it on the
table, and lay down to sleep, and dreamed I was talking to you. You
said, "You're much younger than my mother, of course, but you look

like her." You said, "I'm going to kill myself." And I said, "How does
your mother feel about that?" You said, "She's without feelings, very
factual; she says, There's only a fifty-fifty chance you'll pull it off with
this method, they're so good these days at reviving people with money."
"What method, Michael?" And you said, "The broth method." Then
you said, "Did you imagine, when you were a youngster, that in 30 or
40 years you would be my mother, and having this conversation?" I
said, "That's right, it is 30, no, 40 years. I don't want to be in your
mother's shoes right now."

Waking up, I thought: No, this is the other Michael.

Bud

Christmas night, my father said, "Jean,
you are so disloyal." But Bud said,
"No. Ethereal. Ethereal, but my friend.
And I, I *got* my prayer answered:
I died with my life around me."

To a Young Poet

This January night at ten below I wish you
true desire, like a rose: to stand
in your chest. Veined. Bloom.

Let you be. Reflected in the train window,
inside a thousand circles of public darkness,
desire, a round red star.

And desire again, a foliating wand,
and you the Jack of Wands.

The round red rose of sleep in bloom. This is
true desire, it lets you be.
It says, "No money here."

What does it taste like?
True desire. Eye-
shadow, cinnamon.

Foraging

1. THE ROOM
Why did you keep finding me where I was?
Your seeking, your cage:
oh, your animus against breasts, shadowed eyelids . . .
yet like holding your breath, holding Love.

Love, you said,
come in. Love, let me in.
Everyone else was asleep.
Look at me, you said.

The luminous room.
Eve formalized.

A kiss: my fear and
my love,

not here yet,
but *for* here.

2. THE LUMINOUS ROOM
What it felt like:
first it was the kiss.
Look at me, he said.

And then it was the floor,
the boards. He went slow, he'd
pull and pull and pull at my leaf thirst.

Or running backwards he'd wind the kite-string lace
down out of me so the hot slow wind
would almost touch me . . . No . . . Then God,
the first room: sky, and trees,
but water: blue blue blue bloom bloom.
It was the feeling of terrible scarcity
and then it was the boards
and then it was the luminous room.

Alfred and the Abortion

Alfred, what did they do with your arm bones?
Burned, lying in ashes and clinkers,

or long arm bones lying inwards
Christian-folded fallen across your dropped
rib bones, out there on Long Island . . .

Your heavy right wrist bones
that engineered your work:
a rose, a rainbow of oil on the rowboat floor:

the baby we lost in sixty-nine, with you
in the hospital out of work when I did it
and I couldn't have told you then. Her name was Gift.

Twenty years later I dreamed last night of your wrist,
me eating your wrist, for the child to eat it,
your hand working, and the virtue of your wrist.

Redemption

Nan, the poet in Rome, New York, yesterday
wrote she saw the word "Confluence" in her sleep.

The run of black hair down your arm,
the deep-worn line across your polished shoe.

"Confluence": two rivers joining,
or, the longing to return:

because Jim, we parted
on either side of this green island,
it seems it was a hundred years ago.

But now there is no inside wall:
all down our bodies, from our heads to our feet,
there's only a line like light,
and all around us
a line like an eggshell of light.

Seeing You

I. MOTHER
I was born under the mudbank
and you gave me your boat.

For a long time
I made my home in your hand:

your hand was empty, it was made
of four stars, like a kite;

you were afraid, afraid, afraid, afraid,
I licked it from your finger-spaces

and wanted to die.
Out of the river sparks rose up:

I could see you, your fear and your love.
I could see you, brilliance magnified.

That was the original garden:
seeing you.

2. LOVER
Your hand was empty, it was made
of four stars, like a kite;

blessed I stood my fingers
in your blue finger-spaces, my eyes' light in

your eyes' light,
we drank each other in.

I dove down my mental lake fear and love:
first fear then under it love:

I could see you,
Brilliance, at the bottom. Trust you

stillness in the last red inside place.
Then past the middle of the earth it got light again.

Your tree. Its heavy green sway. The bright male city.
Oh that was the garden of abundance, seeing you.

The Free Abandonment Blues

Now I don't have to leave this place not for anybody
No I don't have to go out of this wooden house not to oblige anybody
Once I would have lifted clean out of my own place to please
    somebody

The blue-robed man who said You want to be loved, love me
The man in the blue robe who said I give, in order that you will give
to me
I remember you my old blue-robed man, but you know this just can
not be

Now if I want to warm myself I look up at the blue sky
Now I look to a number of people here and also to the round blue sky
To feel the sun, your free mouth on my mouth, not the fire that is
gone by

I don't wear any clothes nowadays or say that I am me
I don't wear the right clothes in the closet or explain how I am me
I come as I go translucent oh what you get is what you see

The woman said:
They held her in their arms and knew that she would save them
They brought her into their houses and into their hands to save them
But secretly they knew that no one would ever have them

And she said,
Listen, it's only a little time longer to wait
When you have taken this path you need just a little more time to
wait
Maybe not today the amazing loveliness but it won't be long for us to
wait

The First Station

The first silver work of kindness,
my hand, your hand and your eye, and then the gold play

of watery car lights across the child's white quilt
we slept under and on top of, that February . . .

The rude walnut smell of the hibernation nest.
Sleeping I thought

If there was a hole through you
and a hole through me
they'd take the same
peg or needle
and thread us both
through the first station
and there we'd lean
and listen and listen . . .

Night Lake

He must have been one or two, I was five,
my brother Johnny's cock
floated like a rose of soap in the tub;
it had the faint, light rock of the boat
you carry in you when you're on land again
at the end of the day . . .

Oh all I've never gotten written down!
On paper, on my skin. Oh navy blue lake
that I want to drink
to the bottom. And you,
Barrie, what can I give you to drink?
Not the flask of ourselves, we already have that.

The solitude drink
in the kerosene lamplight at the caravan table . . .

The Badlands Said

I am the skull
under your hundred doubts. I, I
will be with you always.
Heart's-deprive.
Still numinous and alive.
Elephant's side.

Come lie down,
tooth and bone.

Ya, ya,
from a mile high
I crook you up warm,
rabbit-arm.

I am love's sorrow,
the desert's violet needle and gray star.

The Missouri Speaks

for Jonathan Dunn, 1954–1988
Wolf Creek, Montana

Jonathan,
I am the pearl
The pearl at the node of the net of all the worlds

The jewel at the crown of your head
Turquoise

Ivory embryo
Spiral I bide

Sow and reap
Bale and step

Sow bread
Reap bread

Powerless I promise
Fire and bones and flesh

All I give I will sheave.

The River at Wolf

Coming east we left the animals
pelican beaver osprey muskrat and snake
their hair and skin and feathers
their eyes in the dark: red and green.
Your finger drawing my mouth.

Blessed are they who remember
that what they now have they once longed for.

A day a year ago last summer
God filled me with himself, like gold, inside,
deeper inside than marrow.

This close to God this close to you:
walking into the river at Wolf with
the animals. The snake's
green skin, lit from inside. Our second life.

The Ring

The ring was
three times too small for a finger,

even a piece of string could not go through it!
So I asked her,
Woman, why have you sold or given me this ring?
Nunlike she bobbed her white head-scarf chastisingly,
black eyes, black under her eyes, she said,
Something is being taken away.
You must keep seeing: everything
must be turned to love that is not love.
Mother,
going in to death,
can you do it: love
something that was there that is being taken away.

Barrie's Dream, the Wild Geese

"I dreamed about Elizabeth Bishop
and Robert Lowell—an old Penguin book
of Bishop's poetry—a thick china cup
and a thick china sugar bowl, square,
cream-colored, school stuff.
                   And Lowell was there,
he was talking and talking to us,
he was saying, 'She is the best—'
Then the geese flew over,
and he stopped talking. Everyone stopped talking,
because of the geese."
              The sound of their wings!
Oars rowing, laborious, wood against wood: it was
a continuing thought, no, it was a labor,
how to accept your lover's love. Who could do it alone?
Under our radiant sleep they were bearing us all night long.

Fox Glacier

The Tourist: Blue plough bones
               High eye socket
               Soot rock gristle
               Be with me
               Be with me
               Be with me
               Never be not with us
               Fox

The Glacier: My gentle coming: fall
               I am with you my
               Gold-pan
               My sieved and sieving brow
               Most wanted: Favorite:
               Wanted and needed and loved: Diaspora.

Lindis Pass, Borage

in memory of Patricia Walsh

Mary
when you swam up (in reality rose,
assumed) to feed on bliss:
that rounder reality:
you left your dress blue borage like a painted dress
permanent violet cobalt ultramarine and white
lighting this chainlink gate;

open for Pat:
ten children, emphysema, dead at forty:
"Too good for this world."

Open for me! I slam against the gate
dumber than any sheep. I want, I want.
I want to become round like you there: like God: reality:
not flat like here, all oil, all pleasantness and heat.

By the Tekapo River, 100 Degrees

Water
Hot green plastic bucket
Hole
Rabbit in the wall of the ground
Bone
Rabbit, hip, shoulder
Leaf   under a leaf of dust

On my way to wash,
the heavy buzz of flies like bees:
there's a carcass here. Rabbit. Eels
live to be ninety . . . An eel will eat your hand.

I smell the past: where you swam with me,
not toothed as you are, but as you were,
safe in your first, soft shirt.

After Consciousness of This Big Form

Sam and I chose a workshop called
"Fruitfulness." At the round door
a beautiful leader met us, smiling.
Many people pooled into the room,
they opened their arms and they rolled their heads around,
like an old musical, opened their arms and rolled their heads around:

"When I get up in the morning,
after consciousness of this big form . . ."

Maybe so-and-so would like a child,
but I am too old to give birth. Too old,
too much wanting to live my life, not take care
of anyone as so-and-so takes of so-and-so.
When I get up in the morning I am water and wine
with this big form, this pouring out spiral of stars . . .

Everyone Was Drunk

South Dakota, August 1989. The buffaloes' deep red-brown
hinged shoulders and beards, their old hinged humps . . .
These are the old males, separated from the herd.
You can get a state license to shoot them.

"So who saved me? And for what purpose?"

The rich WASP suburb, 1946. The fight
about the Jews on Wall Street. My uncle said,
I thought that's what we fought the war about.
My uncle was right; everyone was drunk; my mother
was peeling shivers of Scotch tape off the counter, peeling off
her good hope. Or was it I who was losing my hope? in the
violent lightning white on the white lawn.
So why was I handed out of the burning window?
For joy. Journalism. Stories.

In Fear (1)

By the St. Vrain River
thirty cars, thirty young men

looking down into the water.
What are they looking at? Now the police cars.
What is going to happen? Now the ambulances.
Someone was here and is gone.

In Fear (2)

M. comes and hits me,
along the spine,
top to bottom,
karate-handed.
I say, It hurts me! And she,
her face the face of a person
in Hell, compelled to unhappy action:
"It hurts everyone."

In This Egg

My mother as a child
under her father's sexual hand
ticking over her like an electric train.
The household scissors to her hair.

Scissors cut paper
Paper covers rock
Rock crushes scissors

Sticks and fluttering paper notes
gravestones   river stones
scissors   holocaust.

My mother and her father, in this blue egg.
This egg, our young, gone before us:
who will brood over them?
Who will make a good roof over them.

The Under Voice

I saw streaming up out of the sidewalk the homeless women and men
the East side of Broadway fruit and flowers and bourbon
the homeless men like dull knives gray-lipped the homeless women
connected to no one streaming no one to no one
more like light than like people, blue neon,
blue the most fugitive of all the colors

Then I looked and saw our bodies
not near but not far out,
lying together, our whiteness

And the under voice said, Stars you are mine,
you have always been mine; I remember the minute on the birth table
when you were born, I riding with my feet up in the wide silver-blue
    stirrups,
I came and came and came, little baby and woman, where were you
    taking me?
Everyone else may leave you, I will never leave you, fugitive.

Come Akhmatova

A homeless woman with harsh white hair
stands outside my Chinese-red door

blocking my way into my
home place:
She says *I lived here once.*
This was my place. I want my pictures.

I have them, the glass of the frames is broken,
if she comes in
she will be my bad ikon,
throw me away
as I throw her away, her
gray unmoving accusing stare. Come Akhmatova
in the siege of Leningrad:
"Can you write about this?" "I can."

James Wright: in Memory

Looking back at me
from his death, from the feminine side, he asks me
to touch him on his throat, on his breastbone,
to touch the spots that have the life in them. His voice
is closer to me than I am to myself.
Unknowable, beginning in joy, his voice
is closer to me than I am to myself.

Wish-Mother

I've never felt
so close to you, Wish-Mother. Wings, oh
my black darling. Almost free.
Never felt so close to anyone. Felt,
Hide you in the shelter of my wings.

All the way home to New York my heart hurt.
Am I taking the old glass out of the frame? Are we?

I love glass because of water,
water because of blood,
blood because of your heart,
lapping against the birth door to my ear,
over and over, my darling, my familiar. And my good.
All the way home to New York my heart hurt.
(The second time you died this year.)

At Cullen's Island

in memory of Eimear Cullen,
1983–1990

Eimear was dead:
Every rock was a green womb, lit from inside.
The trees were like big soft women
whose mossy hooves
burned at the touch of the earth:
Eimear was dead:
Every rock was a green womb, lit from inside.

The Wisdom Gravy

Goosedown on the warm curve of a pail.
Hundreds of young rooks flying into the tree.
John: *I'd like to get good at it, at being married.*
Me: *Well you can't do better than that.*
John: *She thinks I can do much better, than talk about wanting!*
I said to her, I know I haven't done well

these last two years, these first few years,
but I want to get good at it. I'm good at being alone.

A.'s jealousy. B.'s jealousy. Of life.
All night I sucked at wisdom like a shooting tooth:
this morning life's a light garment, a garment of light,
like in our paradise. A. keeps the manger, B. keeps it too, forever
and ever. This gravy is wide and deep, saltier and stranger,
I've carried it home to you under my white hat.

American River Sky Alcohol Father

What is pornography? What is dream?
American River Sky Alcohol Father,
forty years ago, four lifetimes ago,
brown as bourbon, warm, you said to me,
"Sorry sorry sorry sorry sorry."
Then: "You're killing your mother."
And she: "You're killing your father."
What do men want? What do fathers want?
Why won't they go to the mothers?
(What do the mothers want.)
American River Sky Alcohol Father,
your warm hand. Your glass. Your bedside table gun.
The dock, the water, the fragile, tough beach grass.
Your hand. I wouldn't swim. I wouldn't fly.

The Morning of My Mother's Death

A thumbnail-sized globe of blood:
an embryo:
I lose it, I can't find it.

A woman, a midwife or a companion,
says, do I *want* her to kill it?

Our mother wants to take herself
away from us. My kisses.
She loves another country
better than this.
Another class of people.
The class of the dead.

Listen listen listen:
(whisper this:)
her silk spirit is leaving the crown of her head.

The Night of My Mother's Death

The night of my mother's death:
what I saw:

They are winding a bandage all around her head. I say,
Leave holes for her eyes and her mouth.
Then I look down, and I see,
my own wrist is only a spine of bones.

Then how will I listen any more?

I ask you Davoren Hanna, and you say:
"Ordinary communication is too slow
to succinctly indicate
my meaning."

I ask you Emily Dickinson,
water-spider rowing over danger and death: four white lines,
four white lines: nothing over nothing.

Second Mother

Black hair,
and the white hill,
and the one cedar tree, "like a soldier,"

the ripe hot stench of your motorcycle,
its squatting gleam . . .

Then, by the river,
Ha! Ha! I could have touched
your bright white circles,
your nipples' little red mouths,
redder than my mother's.

Black Hair, Black Hair! I was four, you were
sixteen, seventeen, half-girl, half-mother,
you held out safety like a sugar cube,
but how could I get to suck on it? in this world . . .

The Sea of Serenity

The Sea of Serenity:
my mother's body: ashes:
the appearance of land, and the appearance of water.

Books by the fireplace: gold brocade and silver:
but love, oh love. Outside the door.

Earth said, *Eat.*
Earth said, *Shame.*

Mother,
on my hands and knees,
face flat in the leaves,
I chomp after you like a horse.

Who died?
Who died?
Who died?

My Mother's Body, My Professor, My Bower

Who died? My mother's body,
my professor, my bower,
my giant clam.
Serene water, professor
of copious clay,
of spiraling finger-holes in the clay,
of blue breast-milk,
first pulse, all thought:
there is nothing to get. You can't eat money,
dear throat, dear longing,
dear belly, dear fatness,
dear silky fastness: ecstatic lungs' breath,
you can't protect yourself,
there is nothing to get.

Butane

The huge aluminum airship
is gliding over us,
you and I with our children walking by Westport's
trees, seashore, gold trees, gold seashore.
I say, *What's that?* But no one sees it.
Then the second ship crashes just behind us,
spills butane lighter fluid over the field,
thinly spreading, fast, out over the next field;

we don't know, should we throw water over it
or not—which will be worse for the earth
(the earth itself isn't on fire yet,
only the corn in the field, and the next field).
The dwarf says, *Hold it!* walking up between my legs
into my body: *I'd better see the fire skin.*

At My Mother's Grave

Being told,
Go away.

So what is left?
This dark space on the road, that was a deer.
So many gifts:
her hazel eyes . . .

What day did she go away?

Walt Whitman,
visitor,
Emily Dickinson,
canoe of light,
Pablo Neruda,
radio flier,
fly me in.

We Go Through Our Mother's Things

When we started that day
to paint snow for earth

and sky for bread
then we knew it was time to light the last candle.
This ring is yours.   This lamp.

Death Asphodel

—I feel like I've buried somebody inside of me
   Parts of her
   I don't remember yet
   Parts of myself I don't remember yet

—Yes you mean
   there is somebody blind and gummy
   lying next to you when you're asleep

—Yes that's it. Goodbye,
   down the elevator,
   something about flowers,
   about giving flowers. Me
   to my daughter?
   My daughter to me?
   My mother to me. Green flowers soon to bloom.

To the Memory of David Kalstone

Here's the letter I wrote,
and the ghost letter, underneath—
that's my work in life.

The First Angel

Fat slippery angels,
two by two,
carrying sheaves of straw
to the graveyard,
leaning sheaves of straw
on the gravestones,
straw on the frost stones.

God's hands trembled when he
touched my head,
we are so much in love:
the new moon holding the old moon in her arms.

The first angel said, Write down this:
It is time to leave your past life, leave your plumb-line, your trowel,
your layers of habitation, your perfect finds-tray.

At the Door

Seeing my daughter in the circle of lamplight,
I outside:

It is not *I*,
it is *Mother.*
(But it is *I.*)

It is the first tableau, the first
red wellspring of *I.*

Chimpanzee of longing,
outside the light,

wrap your long arms
around the globe of light,
hold your long haunches
wide open: be
ungodly I.

Yield Everything, Force Nothing

Years circling the same circle:
the call to be first,
and the underlying want:

and this morning, look! I've finished now,
with this terrific red thing,
with green and yellow rings on it, and stars.

The contest is over:
I turned away,
and I am beautiful: Job's last daughters,
Cinnamon, Eyeshadow, Dove.

The contest is over:
I let my hands fall,
and here is your garden:
Cinnamon. Eyeshadow. Dove.

Alone, Alive

Alone, alive
with you

more alone
more alive
open open
to and from
the bloodwarm breast
the nest you were born to
the eye the hair
the window the light. Light
the astronauts saw
and grew full of trepidation,
softer,
and more full of life.

My window
my cove
my trout
my flood
my green trepidation
my mushroom
my tongue
my salt my moon
my moon my sun
I lay down my
spear
before your light
your eye
your hair.

Flower

You, I, steadying
in our in-borne, out-borne sparks
of empathy, the flower
of Earth: wet red fireworks-flower.

Skate

Now a year after your death, fish-mother, skate,
you swim up off the surface of the earth:
your other-worldly face
not saying anything
face I can never meet
inside the inside face
not since the land came wet
out of the water, face
under all the pieces of light,
how could I get to you?
Never leave you. Please you!
Teacher, spine in my spine:
the spelling of the world
kneels down before the skate.

Guardian Angel in New York

You stood in the doorway in the snow:
Times Square, a late hour.
The sill was black with chicken's blood:
your black boots open: your glasses like O's:
you touched your finger to your lips, you said,
Here: Wisdom. Wisdom and power.

To Plath, to Sexton

So what use was poetry
to a white empty house?

Wolf, swan, hare,
in by the fire.

And when your tree
crashed through your house,

what use then
was all your power?

It was the use of you.
It was the flower.

The Power Table

You, lying across the wide bed, vertical,
I, horizontal,

you, I, in a green field two green paths
flowered with xxxx's and xxxx's

you, I, lined inside
with pre-historic quarrels

old black cuts
in a wooden kitchen table

the table where you sit down with your older brothers
the table where things get settled once & for all

the cow's hip shaved down to the brand
her body divided into zones

Yes I am standing in the doorway
yes my softness & my hardness are filled with a secret light,

but I want world-light
and this-world company.

Growing Darkness, Growing Light

(1997)

I . . . like to deal with the relationship between growing darkness and growing light, the dusk and the dawn, those times when there is a chance to see transition . . . The dream is a connection, another transitional time. An example would be light coming into the world at dawn. In dreams we sometimes can see resemblances of where we really came from, whether we can explain it or not.
—Lance Henson, in Joseph Bruchac's *Survival This Way,*
Interviews with American Indian Poets

Rain

Snakes of water and light in the window
snakes that shrug out of their skins and follow
pushing a path with their heads full of light
—heavy trembling mercury headlights—
leaving trails of clear grass, and rocks,
nests where they half live, half sleep,
above ground:
Snake where do you come from?
who leave your grass path
and follow me wordless
into our glass
water and light house,
earth wet on your mouth,
you the ground of my underground.

Sick, Away from Home

My head
the Jenny Lind's head,
the painted tall ship's figurehead:
full, staring eyes,
beautiful:
but instead of the prow's wood at her back,
at my back a Monarch wing,

and the head and the wing
held up not by her wooden neck
and breasts of wood
but by an upright, silent thumb:
dream thumb
                —me dreaming
over the wet electric New York streets.

Friend

Friend I need your hand every morning
but anger and beauty and hope
these roses make one rose.

Friend I need a hand every evening
but anger and hope and beauty
are three roses
that make one rose.

Let's fix our bed it's in splinters
and I want to stay all year.

Let's fix our bed it's in splinters
and I want to stay all year.

Did you hear what that woman on Grafton Street was saying?

You won't be killed today.
We don't even know we're born.

Homesick

Leonardo's man in the circle, but a woman,
the circle adrift in the middle of the lake:
cross through the line someone, salmon or hawk.

The rowboat drifts
on this northern evening's midnight line of light,
green lip reflecting lip,
and I float in it,
salt, and breath, and light,
hawk and salmon and I . . .

New Life

B. walks around with a fire-box inside his chest.
If you get near him it will burn you too. B. says

Don't let the women go out of our lives like the swallows
leaving only the crows' liquid leathery reign, domain, stain.

I love B.   And I love my life.
The taste of my own life is good to me. New life.
My skin.   And B.'s fire skin.

Bees

A man whose arms and shoulders
and hands and face and ears are covered with bees
says, *I've never known such pain.*
Another man comes over
with bees all over his hands—
only bees can get the other bees off.
The first man says again,
I've never known such pain.
The second man's bees begin to pluck
the first grave yellow bees off, one by one.

The Tractors

The tractors at night,
the dimly lighted
kindly lobsters
with glass sides,

with men inside,
and at home, wives,
and depression's black dogs
walking out of
the January hedges'
hacked-off sides.

River Jordan

O mud mother lick me before I die
before I'm only
a wooden case of disintegration
disowned things

and then—after this life—
the scar part, the lily, the rose *not* descending?
the eagle above the Wyoming
road? with six-foot wings outspread . . .

—No, not your mother either, this is me
the one who kissed you on your lips, your
nose, your stomach (secretly!), who carried you, it's me
who you belong to in reality.

Night Porch

Back home, after a month away
leaning on my night porch

what had I come to? out of air,
nose at the glass: to this gold dress

Nose at the glass: sweet inside world
where there was enough, enough, enough

And here was my husband
the grazer-beside, the distance sharer

but not he, or I, but the inside angel
held open the glass door, and led us led us . . .

*

World-light

Do well in the world.

If you do well
we'll throw you away.

We'll put you in the state asylum
like we did your grandfather.

(He did well then fell.)
("The drink." "But harmless.")
   But if you fall

we'll never say your name.
They'll think you're dead.

You will be one of the
Disappeared.

(We too, although we live
on a certain street, have certain jobs,

we too, we were
the Neverhere.)

Snow Family

Snow family: big snow father,
coal eyes, coal teeth,

small snow mother, no mouth,
smaller and smaller snow daughters,

and over them, a red felt banner:
I LIKE MY WOMEN'S VOICES SOFT.

And who were the child wife, husband, Mother
Father? King Queen? Brother? Never

to know. The snow
streamed upward
into the scree . . .

To the Black Madonna of Chartres

Friend or no friend,
darkness or light,
vowels or consonants,
water or dry land,

anything more from you now
is just gravy
—just send me down forgiveness, send me down
bearing myself a black cupful of light.

Tell Me, What Is the Soul

There is a prison room,
the floor, cement,
in the middle of the room
a black pool full of black water.
It leads to an invisible canal.
Plunder is the pool. Plunder is the canal.

By the wall,
by a fire,
Mandelstam was reciting,
in his yellow leather coat,
the criminals were listening,
they offered him
bread and the canned stuff,
which he took . . .

Mastectomy

for Maura

They used to make a new breast for you
—no you made it: for who, for who—
with a bag of birdseed.

What happened to your breast?
No good to eat,

no good for love,
hungry hungry.

In a forest fire you make a fire
the size of yourself,
let it go out,
and lie in it.

I am hungry for my own heart. Heart's
work is normal harsh and sweet: throw out the
hospital bracelet, the hiding sheet.

Secret Room, Danger House

—Secret Room, Danger House:
the place where my belly
and my bone shelf meet:

Secret Room, Danger House:
dirty red inside:

—No it's clear, ruby red,
red as this ring
I give thee love.

Red for Blood

My sister comes around the corner of the house
carrying two bloody lambs, new-born
or hurt, I don't know, Eternity,
they beam blood.

They beam blood.
A little boy
comes down the chimney to bring me back
up with him. Covered with soot.

I don't want to go,
but I can't not go,
the animals all
go up like chimney-sweeps, Eternity,
you, me, up on a rope like the live geese,
chimney-sweep geese.

Yellow for Gold

Begging my mother to speak to him,
I pleaded my silent father's cause.

I pleaded my cause with my daughter.
My my my
my baby my Solomon also.

I bought a coconut boat
from a Rastafarian man: he said,
This boat is red for blood,
yellow for gold, green for the land,
black for the people.

Nightbook, nightboat of lights.

Where does my gold come from,
Solomon? Freely given, freely
taken away. Fly, father, daughter, fly.

Green for the Land

Because why — I was dis-
similar —

they staked my feet,
tied my hands,
threw me in,
but I stuck, I
caught on the side,
they see:
I lived.

No more room on the pages
of my green book to write on,
and someone coming back
wanting me: thief
of my land, my childhood thief.

Black for the People

The man I am with is black,
we are with nothing but white men.
He's caught, he says
they're going to shock him or burn him.
I say I'll be there.

But I'm not him.
He has to go into a machine where
two white men put him. The machine
saws loud into his back, three,
four inches, into his back.
Then they let him go. Not

wanting him alive, not wanting him dead.
Their knees grind over the sea
and make malice. What is love? What does love do.

Home

Breath entering, leaving the leaf,
the lion tense on the branch luxuriant,

the ten-foot drop to
the water-hole, the God-taste

— *that's* what lights it up,
Nature, and Art: your skin feather to feather
scale to scale to my skin

and the airy sleep, like wine . . .
two soft old children's books
with the red and blue and green crayons still warm on us.

Long Irish Summer Day

A lorry scatters
hay down the road
red as blood.

Down by Tommy Flynn's
a young man is sowing
in the ten o'clock sunset

sowing salt tears on the road
— not for the ice, we already have sand.

Sun and moon shine into our glass room,
two countries, two cities,
two glass houses:
a shotgun is hanging on the wall.

*

Dog Skin Coat

in memory of Lynda Hull

Lynda, the third, last time we talked
we talked about Mandelstam's yellow leather coat
—you told me "it was dog skin."

Ghost money, star
ledger, I'm hanging his yellow coat up here
on your coffin-door:

They'd skin a dog for a coat,
but why skin you?
Why skin a car?
Red open boat, why you?

Three nights after you died I dreamed we were thrown
out of a car. I said, "Lynda, come on, get over to the side."
You laughed, the way you'd laugh to a child, you said
"You only want to drink the gasoline."

Lynda, it wasn't dog skin.
He told his wife he wouldn't wear a coat
made out of "man's best friend."
Ghost star, is there a dog there? Any friend?

Fellini in Purgatory

He was shoveling sand
at the edge of the water, his heavy black glasses
glittered with rain:

"Don't you see how much like a woman I am?"
Shovel, shovel.

His throat was wrapped in water,
and the water flowered with milt.

Shoveler, are you eating the earth?
Earth eating you?

Teach me
what I have to have
to live in this country.

And he, as calm as calm, though he was dead:
"Oh, — milt, — and we're all of us milt."

Elegy for Jane Kenyon

The rooks rise off the field in a black W
and break up, black Cassiopeia breaking up

at the hour of your death. Your music is broken
and eaten among the American poets

and you are gone,
angry wolf, sad swallow,
and you are gone,
blest boat, blest water,
gone in the first hour
and gone in the second hour . . .

You Are Not One in a Sequence

Here
Child
who is to die
take this breast
this rattle this dress
don't listen to your friends
on the other side . . .

Child who is dead:
you are not one in a sequence.
Don't come back,
blush on your cheek,
do not push your white boat up to our dock.
Let you: stay over there, with your heaven-dog and your friends,
and we: drop back down into our intents.

Alcohol

At a memorial service
in a high school auditorium
M. in her raincoat: she

turns my hand over in hers,
she says, At *least we had July.*

Never, never, and she is gray, transparent,
fragile, made of
dusty glass,

Gilbey's Gin,
the Glass Flowers . . .

Where Do You Look for Me?

in memory of James L. White

They think because I am dead now
I am no longer twigs on the ground,
stones or bits of stone in the wall.
That I was just something good on a plate
for them to eat. That I have no one.

Oh my darling,
where do you look for me?

Documentary: AIDS Support Group

White paper masks over their mouths
—a piano player; an artist;
the others I don't know.

A hot light bulb, the childhood smell
of a Magic Lantern. The artist shows a slide:
closeup cracks like rivers in the leather of an armchair.

"We learned before this to read the cracks of fever,
at nine, and one, and five," the artist says.
The flat deflection of the piano player's eyes.

Poem with Words by Thornton Dial

Day by day you are being drawn
through the TV's violet needle's eye.

Luminous is the hope you have been content with.

The shaman breaks the wrist of his
countryman to get him to talk.
The film crew walk around at the edge.

A guru beams in his jazz musician's shades.

Luminous is the hope you have been content with.
— *Graveyard traveler,*
I am coming in.

A Bit of Rice

A bit of rice in a string bag:
the rice spills,
we have to sweep it up . . .
What will be left here when you die?
Not the rice
not the tea
left *somewhere* when the monk

knocked over the cup
not
not

The Night of Wally's Service, Wally Said,

"Most people will reflect back to you
however they feel about themselves,
but you have to say Hey,
don't look at me that way,
I'm only one day dead,
I need care.
                              But not Mark,
who looks at you with love.
No matter what. Like today, in church,
I was off somewhere, off Provincetown,
most people wanted me to come back,
but not Mark."

Rodney Dying

R. is sitting in a draft
—we trade places.
I see that he has a large, round hole
from the top of his head
down into his belly,
a tunnel with blood and bones around it.
He is himself,
not pretending
but completely courteous and sweet. He says,
You have to wrap your feet with paper
from now on
for this new journey.

Rodney Dying (2)

Dancing in a room full of muzak and smoke
me with my sixty years of rings
inside my fingers like trees
with this breath which is mine
and is yet not mine
—but my friend is dying
and there's nothing I can do
in this pure blue country.
And a voice from outside the blue window said,
"Everything is sad except what's real."

Father Lynch Returns from the Dead

There's one day a year
they can return,
if they want.
He says he won't again.
I ask what it's like—
he quotes St. Paul:
"Now hope is sweet."
Then in his own voice:
Oh well it's a great scandal,
the naked are easier to kill.

The Baby Rabbits in the Garden

—Our mother laid us there
in grass and hair.
The tunnel fell,
the farmer's boot arrived

and put us out,
too poor to stay alive.

—And now the farmer too with his large white head
backwards or forwards by a belt is led
down the black hall
hungerless to bed

and soon will the reader too
my listening head
be laid to bed,
the tunnel fall . . .

*

Mother and Child, Body and Soul

Child
You've boarded me over like a window or a well.

Mother
It was autumn
I couldn't hear the students
only the music coming in the window,
Se tu m'ami
If you love me

I went for a week's journey in soft ermine.
Darling, the ovals of your hair . . .

autumn leaves,
your hair the hue of rain-drenched bark, your voice:

Don't ever leave me . . .

And this child, this
window in my side,
boarded over all my life,
—how can I take the boards off, in this wind?
I will break if I bend . . .

Soul

I—as daughter—am black:
I—mother—shun her,
keep her out of everything.

The daughter says, *I'm anorexic,*
don't think I don't like the meat.   She says,

I don't want to be an animal.   Animals
eat other animals.

She is my soul
saying

You will never know me.
Beginning to talk.

Soul (2)

Lying in a bunk on a train
almost crushed by the woman above

strong red lipstick
big red smile

though she seems asleep. My mother is bleeding
out of the two sides of her spine,

I am putting ice on it. Freud says,
'The private is a gunbarrel.'

M. and me: two panes of glass
without even air between them.

The Mother Dreams

I'm with D. and a young woman
going into my New York apartment.
I say *It's a long time since I've been here,*
I don't know what it will look like,

— In the hall: an umbilical cord.
An aborted baby.

But it can't be mine,
I haven't been here . . .

In the next room
there are two babies
the room is flooding

the two babies are floating but soon
the water will rise.
One baby puts her finger in a socket

it catches fire
she puts it in the water.
The other is nursing from a bottle

and will drown. I take the babies
and look for help. There is none.
The medical guy leaves for home.

I saw and I did nothing.
I knew and I did nothing.

Fistula

The blood rushing under her
inside elbow skin

"Here, feel it"
rushing towards me

speeded-up water
flooding across

the fields of Ireland,
rushing away:

the silence of the mother,
the silence of the child.

Soul (3)

A man with an infant in his lap
whose throat swells up and wrinkles down
like a frog's: the man weeps,

Adapt, Adapt.
— A woman's voice:
"Always the sex-man." Desolate.

Oh my soul, *not* gone away?
When this man's starlight reaches your eye,
your eye is still
here to see . . .

*

Open Heart

1. EMERGENCY ROOM
The lion retreats from the cage we can see
to the cage in the back, dragging the boy who climbed
in. Bone case inside bone case.

Oh sane daylight side-
light these four,
the lion the boy myself the night.

2.
The heart was cut up into pieces
put into a Planters peanut jar
and put back on the shelf.
A bum came along
and thinking it was peanuts
he emptied it out and ate it.

3.
Eyes only

brown eyes painted with kohl
red buffalo painted on the wall

hunted, eaten
hidden in people's mouths

a face looking out from a three-foot thick
fall of bougainvillea

—your soul hides from being led
even by you

4. INTENSIVE CARE UNIT
Your shy body, turned
to silk and bone, thin blue silk
coat for what water . . .

5.
They've made a hole
in B's chest
the size of the woodworm holes
in the sideboard: threaded it
with black plastic thread:
their jump-start track to his heart.

6.
The surgeon said,
"You don't have to visit,
he won't remember it.
Ten minute visits."

Everyone here walks in a deep
open-eyed and rigid sleep.

In this deep
black unfold

we don't know what is happening to us,
no more than the dumb beasts of the field. Do they.

Listening

My whole life I was swimming listening
beside the daylight world like a dolphin beside a boat

—no, swallowed up, young, like Jonah,
sitting like Jonah in the red room
behind that curving smile from the other side

but kept, not spat out,
kept, for love,

not for anything I did, or had,
I had nothing but our inside-
outside smile-skin . . .
my paper and pen . . .

but I was made for this: listening:
"Lightness wouldn't last if it wasn't used up on the lyre."

The Cradle of the Real Life

(2000)

So long as the heaven of *Thou* is spread out over me the winds of causality cower at my heels, and the whirlpool of fate stays its course . . . No deception penetrates here; here is the cradle of the Real Life.

—Martin Buber

Part I

The Pen

The sandy road, the bright green two-inch lizard
little light on the road

the pen that writes by itself
the mist that blows by, through itself

the gourd I drink from in my sleep
that also drinks from me

—Who taught me to know instead of not to know?
And this pen   its thought

lying on the thought of the table
a bow lying across the strings

not moving
held

Elegy for Jane Kenyon (2)

Jane is big
with death, Don
sad and kind—Jane
though she's dying
is full of mind

We talk about the table
the little walnut one
how it's like
Emily Dickinson's

But Don says No
Dickinson's
was made of iron. No
said Jane
Of flesh.

Black Wolf

Suffocated in the country
a sheep in my own curtain
wolf curtain!

The black wolf nobody else saw I alone saw
trotting down the lane past our house
—Black Heart! Don't go past our house

don't get lost just when I've found you
just when life is not afraid
any more. Of me. Just when—

(I didn't *need* to hate them. You can't beat a stick.
But nobody else could see what they were like.

See it wasn't all
"on the green hill sheep
kneel and feed")—

Mother Bones

B. is dragging his mother's bones
up the stone stairs

in a bag of grass cuttings.
But you can't grow
grass from cuttings.

They lead me

They lead me to a
"lovely nurse"
"in case B. needs her"
she is   I am
sugary
melt
and disappear

I ask for a dream
about my marriage:
"Ink." Ink. Ink. Ink.

My ink-stained hand
his paint-smudged hand

gone   where
nothing joins

Your mouth "appeared to me"

Your mouth "appeared to me"
a Buddha's mouth
the size of a billboard

I thought: of course,
your mouth,
you *spoke* to me.

Then your blue finger,
of course it was your finger,
you painted with your finger

and you painted me with your finger . . .

Then appeared to me flames:
transparencements of every hand and mouth.

Mare and Newborn Foal

When you die
there are bales of hay
heaped high in space
mean while
with my tongue
I draw the black straw
out of you
mean while
with your tongue
you draw the black straw out of me.

Truth

Sharing bread
is sharing life

but truth—
you ought to go to bed at night
to hear the truth
strike
on the childhood clock
in your arms: the
cold house
a turned-over boat,
the walls
wet canvases . . .

October Premonition

October premonition

seeing my friend leave
I turn my head up, away

if she has to leave
let me not see her

my leaving mother
leaving my door open a crack
of light   crack of the depression world

Rodney Dying (3)

I vacuumed your bedroom
one gray sock
got sucked up   it was gone

sock you wore on your warm foot,
walked places in, turned,
walked back

took off your heavy shoes and socks
and swam

November

November
leaving Ireland

Sligo Bay and the two mountains
the female and the male
walking down the stairs
into the ground

—I have to leave
and I have to watch.

Labrador

Crossing a fenced-off railroad track
holes in the fence
carrying a dog
my journey
I drop him
he's heavy   I can't pick him up

he puts his foot in a trap
chained to the track   a trap

yes   but that dog
won't chew his foot off
he's barking at himself   he won't let
me near.
          I left him.

1945

A year in the Pacific
watching his pilots
not come back to the ship

—they were nineteen, twenty,
they called him "Pop" . . .

We lived
for the day he came back.
The day he came back

he raged like Achilles

the day   the year   years

we flew off

one off a bridge   one into a book
one a note
into a bottle

we never came back.

—Oh my dead father
—Ah Jeanie, you're still in words . . .

Leaving

The dark black line
around the darker brown
ball of your eye

—I could only look at one eye at a time
like a horse:
white ring around the eye:

terror.
Eight years I sat on my heels in the field

waiting for you.
I *wanted* to.

Running for a train

Running for a train
an older woman on my back
another old poor woman
needs help to make it too
but I can't help her too
the train has started already
the engineer
is a young woman   she
looks out the window implacably
and keeps on driving
                        I knew her
I knew the old poor woman
still back at the other end of the platform
the woman slipping from me   I knew
the moon-faced boy watching by the side of the tracks

The Welsh poet

The Welsh poet
said of his mother
who "left the world"
last week
"She was never dead
in or out of it."
He shows me a beautiful Indian bird
red with yellow dots on it:
Happiness.   Beauty.   Art.
—That bird seems to like you.
—Yes, that bird knows
there's not much time.
The mother has a gold body now.

Radio: Poetry Reading, NPR

I heard your voice on the radio
thirty years dead
and got across the kitchen to
get next to you
breath and breath
two horses

But it wasn't you back then
I was liquid to,
it was my life:
I wanted to *be* you.
Amount to something. Be

the other
the ready stone
—prayer-rag tied to a wire fence, a branch . . .

The Tower Roof

No music
no memory
not all your art
not   not
your iron story
can fold you into the galaxy

saved by yourself
lost by yourself

your iron words
hero and chorus

This far and no farther.

For a Woman Dead at Thirty (2)

In memory
you
go through that
door and go through that
door and go through that
door

cold
dark

and then the way
the sky is lightest
over water

this world lightened

as your words
opened into their third
star-darkness

The Blind Stirring of Love

I rub my hands my cheeks
with oil   my breasts
I bathe my genitals, my feet
leaf and bark

redden my mouth to
draw down your mouth
and all along
you have been inside me
streaming
unforsakenness . . .

Little Map

The white pine

the deer coming closer

the ant
in my bowl
—where did she go
when I brushed her out?

The candle
—where does it go?

Our brush with each other

—two animal souls
without cave
image
or
word

The Drinker

You   breathless
Drinking   drinking

making for the door
out of your life

heading out through the
chimney   the body-hole

out from the house   the skin and
bone   out from

the silence
—Love

won't take you out   death
won't take you out

nothing that's the same
will take you out

The Drinker (2)

In the doorway
your face a candle

Your face a white island
between the two currents, between the
falls of your black hair

You who drank your life greedily
hole never filled

Girl-woman who could not
whose lips could not open

Hungry ghost in the doorway

Your bones might as well have flown together and spoken:
Where is she whom my heart loves?

—Oh my darling,
where do you look for me?

Happiness

Remember our happiness?
under us   happiness
under the city
under our fathers' graves   happiness
under this world
under the gospel of the evangelist John:
This is the happiness he leaned his head against.

Happiness (2): The I Ching

(Alone)
"Unconcerned"
"Undaunted"

Sunset
sunrise
pines
hermit thrush

Central Park, Billie Holiday
—Misfortune. No blame

—the boat pond
rises
above the trees

: the dead don't go away
: you   "   "   "

He leaves them:

He leaves them:

No nothing's happening
you   why do you
get angry   cry
why are you leaving Me, he cries:

He turns into a moon
They turn into night bandages
He turns into strips of film
blue with another woman's blue
—loses the blue

Away from you

Away from you,
alone, I *can* come

—a leaf flickers
on the river's light skin

Together
we are two stones like one stone rolling

rolling down on the riverbed   two
light black stones

we have always been here
once we *were* one stone

—the other thing holds us
in its mouth

Child

You are in a blind
desert   child

your "too-muchness" is written
in the Torah

child   it is written
in the pit

written in black fire
on white fire

deer star
black star

third star
who sees

Part II Her Lost Book

I.

Embryo

Still mermaid
inside   her
words only
half gathered

her head still floating
listening   listening
                    to the Real Life

The Women's Prison

The women in the prison
are combing mannequins' heads of hair
for Beauty Care.
It's cold in there
a prison necklace of noose and lies

This bodily tool of governments
the tooth pit   the grave

In the Public Library

In the Public Library
a woman is reading a factory story
several people listening
she gets to the fire

the noise   to the locked doors   the death room
The librarian says she has to stop
it's time for him to close. He closes.

Margaret, d. 1985

At the back of the church
dressed like a bag lady, Margaret
in dark torn clothes
with her old woman smell
with the red open wound on her forehead
maggots in her wound . . .

Third floor walkup on 112th
she may have been there 85 years
the steel door open to
cat shit cat food
human shit human food
ghost dust ghost Margaret

holding tight
to her iron bed
and to empty us
of every illusion of separateness,
on her forehead
the maggots' miner's lamp . . .

At the Conference on Women in the Academy

The young scholar, her weeping finger
the anger reality
under the "social construction of reality"
under the deaf blind TV filmed

broadcast auditorium: the woman talking
in the split-open room
under the room of what we say.

The Orphanage Landing

Goldenbridge, Dublin

We her countrypeople are deep asleep
we meet in the local
and talk in our bread-and-butter
sleep. All night the young girl waits
on the orphanage landing as Sister told her
till She comes   down the stairs
with a strap   with scalding water

In the morning the local doctor
covers the wounds up over and over
("called to the orphanage 71 times
in that year")
                White wolves
run in: *No no this never happened.*
(White wolves in every second house are saying:
This is not happening.)

Reading the Mandelstams

Snow falling the sixth night
on the stone house full of silence
Why can't they drive you both now, tonight
up to the house, light up the house

Lines of ice
in the night window
notes

He Says to Me, In Ireland

He says to me, In Ireland
you've fallen into your destiny.
He says
the teaching and giving readings
night and day
keep him from the void. I say,
But you write about the void. I say,

All these women,
your mother,
two wives, a lover,
have died miserably,
and you have lived to write about it
your history of the world.
Or leave it out.

But I want those women's lives
rage   constraints
the poems they burned
in their chimney-throats
The History
of the World Without Words
more than your silver or your gold art.

What God Said

After she died
her son destroyed her paintings:
incinerator flames: "She wouldn't want anyone
to see this stuff." Then killed himself.

Do not fear your death, for when it arrives

*I will draw my breath and your soul will come to me
like a needle to a magnet.*

St. Mechtilde of Magdeburg

---

*

2.

> *Some of the signs suggest that you feel a leaf or
> other part of a plant. A string leads from the top
> of the sign to the plant.*
> —Braille sign on the Miwok Trail, Muir Woods

* * *

She wrote a book. Lost to us.
Her lost book said,
"Your search to find words
that will devour meaning
will devour you."
                    Her lost book said,
"I spent, and I earned, too:
But my money was no good there."

* * *

If my mother was one
and my sister was one
and my father

was not one
and my brother was not one
what was I?   I followed
the string in the dark. Alone:

* * *

Before the expected street into town
before the ramp Contentment
whose handrails budded long before birth
and grew ahead of me like arms
—I stopped like a horse.

* * *

Something bad is happening.
No one says anything.

One by one
they get up and walk away.

They promised not to know.

Generation to generation,
bone to bone.

Poetry

You, poem
the string I followed blind
to leaf by thick green leaf
to your stem
milky
poem without words
world electric with you

The Church

"Thank you for the food," we said,
it was mashed potatoes, gravy, this
was the place the regular people came,
to go through the regular
funnel. Leaving
I saw————and his red
candle of "find it." My life.

* * *

I couldn't
he couldn't

Father I'm twenty

Whiskey   marriage
Children   whiskey

* * *

Alcohol alcohol alcohol
two children   hungry

depression's lead box
no air to breathe

Our therapist:
"You're married to a brilliant man,
you just have to accept it."

* * *

I was dark and silent.
The therapist said,

"Why don't you wear lipstick?"
To J: "Does she lie on top?" To J:
"Don't *play her role.*
Don't give the children their baths
or feed them."

* * *

The soul has no   'other afternoon'
amiga gold
We   then
bandage her feet
as she steps   down and down
past where her parents pray for her
two still dark figures   kneeling in Gemini

Here there is no language

Drink   cut my wrists
drink take bad pills
into the locked ward   take good pills
can't feel   can't
or speak
or step

doctors looking down a well

The Locked Ward: O.T.

Poster paints, big brushes
like my girls' kindergarten brushes:

I make a big picture, primary colors:
the social workers come like kindergarten teachers
and ask me to explain it, I do, they say,
You don't need to be here.

—Where should I be?

* * *

On the mental floor
I painted a picture of the children
Irreducible   altered
the MISSING children
but it was me missing.
Chewing up the mirror   the mother
was not someone else.

* * *

To the half-way house.
Protestant. I made
maple syrup. My friend moved in
with my husband and children.
The Methodist minister: How many men
do you have in your life.
—Sir   none.

Single Mother, 1966

No money
—the baby birds'
huge mouths

huger than themselves
—and God making
words
words

Abortion Child

I thought:
You live somewhere
deeper than the well
I live down in.
Deeper than anything from me or him.

No but it took me
time to see you, thirty earth years.

3.

To Ireland

By the Granary River
the landlord says,
"All these things—
the lambing—the commonage—
are good—yes—but they are not God."
Looking out over us
with a white and English eye.

* * *

Oh yes they are but
by the Granary River
we shut down seven hundred years.
My mother was in it, and hers, and hers,
my great-grandmother, hers died in the black room,
and her mother, mother to mother,
shut down and opened wrong.

Home

I left my clothes
and books
my skin
a snake
—the only one in the country!
Our sign
life   twice

* * *

Scarab rolling a ball of dung
across the ground
scarab hieroglyph:
to come into being:
scarab rolling with the sun
across the sky
Atlantic

* * *

No one's a house
for me anymore

or me for them
Home   not words but
I know it on my lips
it will come   it will melt
like ice on a stove   and I will drink it.

* * *

You walk across your self
as you walk across a dirt road
crossroads at dusk
and across a field   outsider
a field   and a field
steps go beside you   the sun
crossing a line   sun kind to you   sun you.

* * *

Under
water
look up at the dots of the sun run
along on the other side of the water line

under the white pine
the stars run along
on the other side of the sky's line   no lines

* * *

Snow
falling slow
filling our footprints

writing a word

changing it

night
at the window
two birches, blown together.

* * *

Snow falling
off the Atlantic

out towards strangeness

you
a breath on a coal

Index of Titles and First Lines

About the Author

Jean Valentine won the Yale Younger Poets Award for her first book, *Dream Barker*, in 1965. She is the author of nine books of poetry, including most recently *Growing Darkness, Growing Light* (Carnegie Mellon, 1997), and *The Cradle of the Real Life* (Wesleyan, 2000). Valentine has been the recipient of a Guggenheim Fellowship, and the Shelley Memorial Prize. She has taught at Sarah Lawrence College, New York University, and the 92nd St. Y, and lives in New York City.